5 Things Your Guidance Counselor Didn't Tell You

5 Things Your Guidance Counselor Didn't Tell You

A'ric Jackson

iUniverse, Inc.
New York Bloomington Shanghai

5 Things Your Guidance Counselor Didn't Tell You

iUniverse books may be ordered through booksellers or by contacting:

iUniverse
1663 Liberty Drive
Bloomington, IN 47403
www.iuniverse.com
1-800-Authors (1-800-288-4677)

Because of the dynamic nature of the Internet, any Web addresses or links contained in this book may have changed since publication and may no longer be valid.

The views expressed in this work are solely those of the author and do not necessarily reflect the views of the publisher, and the publisher hereby disclaims any responsibility for them.

ISBN: 978-0-595-46055-7 (pbk)
ISBN: 978-0-595-90354-2 (ebk)

Printed in the United States of America

This book is dedicated to all of those who believed in my dream even during the times when I didn't. Especially to My Loving Parents: Angel & Henry (Mom & Husband), Michael and Tanya (Dad & Wife), My Grandmother "Mother", Aunt Bessie "Auntie", My Sister & Best Friend Angela, My Brother & Best Friend Phillie, Spiritual Brother Derral, Spiritual Sister Sharon, Mentors Byron, Iega, Gary and God Father Elliott.

This book is a physical representation of the love and support that you have shown throughout my life. I am a blessed man to have been blessed with such people as you.

This book is also dedicated to the memory of my Aunt Louise. Thank you so much for giving me that "spunk" that I have today. I Love & Miss you.

Two Words I Must Say ... Thank You

First of all, to my Creator, My God, thank you so much for placing this Dream in me and thank you for allowing me to stand strong and allow it to be birthed out into this world. I am grateful for the dream and purpose you have given me.

To my family: Mom, Dad, Tanya and "Pops"—Words cannot express my appreciation for the love you have shown me from day one. Mom & Dad because of who you are, you have allowed me to be the man I am today. To Mother & Grandpa, from your support in my writing from day one to driving me almost everywhere in the city of Chicago, thank you for knowing that this day would be. I love you. Mommy Dee & Daddy Don, you have no idea of how much I am amazed by who you are as human beings and my grandparents. You have been such an undeniable inspiration in my life. Thank you for your example. Auntie Bessie, I am thankful I am able to say thank you for being you in this form. I love you so much. Uncle Percell, I know I have not always been as great to you as you have been to me. Thank you for being there in my life and thank you for allowing me to find me. Angela, my sister, my friend, my heart ... my love for you is so profound. You have been there all the time even despite our hard moments. If those moments were what got us to where we are today, I would not change anything about our life together. Thank you for you and the other two joys in my life, Amar & Jaylah (My Kids—lol).

To my friends: Phillie, Phillie Phillie! Here it is! Thank you for being such a force and a stand for my greatness. You have no idea how much you being a part of my life has allowed me to grow. Derral & Sharon, I'm at a loss for words. Derral you have been the vocal force and Sharon the quiet force. Thank you for believing in me undoubtedly and I love you both for it. Keyana a.k.a. Becky! You have been such an inspiration in my life and I want to show my love for you. Thanks babe. Wendell, took me long enough huh? You have been with me for some time and I am inspired by the man and the force that you are. Love you man. Byron, wow, what can I say? Thank you for your foresight in the greatness I am. You shined a light on me when I didn't think I could be the force I am. You have been such a stand for me and this book. Thank you. I love you. Iega & Gary—Thank you for your love, support, and providing a space for me to grow and become the force I am today. Both of you are the Epitome of the man I want to be and for that I am thankful. Marc Anthony, thank you for showing me so much about myself. In that you have allowed me to grow into my authentic voice of power, know that I love you much. My sons—D'Angelo, Brandon, Jovan and Andrew. I don't know if any of you have an idea of how much you have encouraged me and inspired me over this last year. A great deal of this book was written as if I was leaving you a guide for your lives. Know that I love each and everyone of you as if you were my biological sons—I love you. To my booking manager Darnell Nolin and Van Lin & The Company, I am so grateful you took me on as your client. I look forward to our growth as we both pursue our dreams and in that, I look forward to the continued friendship. Ms. Terrell Jones—love you so much. You have a way of staying on my case in such a loving way and I thank you for your friendship and commitment to transformation. I'll see you at Valois! To Dr. Stephany Spaulding, thank you so much for your input and helping me to realize that my own voice was more than good enough. I love you and miss you. Katie Behrens, from day one, you have been the greatest support. Thank you for your support and love—Gracias!

To everyone at Dowd, Bloch & Bennett especially Marcia Dowd & Elsa Contreras—I love you. Thank you for providing some of my greatest years and experiences in my life. To my boy and personal inspiration Mawi Asgedom—Man! You happy? LOL! My time has come (I know I know, you were right). Thank you for taking me under your wing and teaching/sharing with me your knowledge no holds barred. I know I have not always done what you said or in some cases it took me years to do it, but you are truly my inspiration. I love you man! To my other inspirations John Alston—thank you for being there for me, I look forward to the future and Keith Harrell—Mr. Fantastic I love you and the work you do. Thanks.

To my family at the Illinois Leadership Seminar—please know that this book was inspired by you. I started my dream on your stage and my life has been fulfilling every since. Special thanks to Jen Dowd for seeing something in me and bringing me to this organization. Kristen, you are amazing. Your belief in me is invaluable. I love you. To my Landmark Family—You constantly touch move and inspire me. Thank you. To all my friends and extended family at the Metro Chicago Area Friendship Movement you have shown genuine friendship. Dwayne & Marshall, thank you for your belief in me. To Michael Armstrong and Strong Men United as 1 thanks for allowing me to be me (LOL). To my First Lutheran Church of Harvey Family especially Pastor Tom, Chris, Unity Singers and even Next Generation, you are such an inspiration to me. One 4 Christ! I LOVE YA'LL! ALL 800 of you! Thanks for listening to me and supporting me along the way. I count it an honor and privilege to be a part of you. To Krave & Vassar Magazines, thank you for allowing me to share my dream, passion and voice with your audiences. My Deeply Rooted Family, especially Deeply Rooted Dance Theater 2, just know that you have constantly allowed me to shine in my purpose. Thank you for that.

Last but not least to each and every student who has ever listened to me and allowed yourself to be touched and inspired by my words, you are the reason I love my life. You allow me to be my Dream and Purpose. Thank you for that blessing. Thank You, Thank You, Thank You. If I missed you, please know that it was not intentional. My life has been graced by some of the greatest people on this earth.

To you I say two things, 1—you have touched my life and 2—there will be a second edition! (Smile).

Who I am is Love, Power & One Making a Difference!

Peace!

This section is a special acknowledgement. Everyone listed below invested in the completion of this book. I say it is a special acknowledgement because their investment of purchasing the book before it was published is a testament of their belief and faith in this project. So I introduce to you

The Dream Believers

Derral Anderson, Jr.

Katie Behrens

Delores & Colton Bentley

The Berridge Family

Robert Bloch

Angie Blunt

Phillip E. Blunt

Sharon Bouie

Keyana Brown

Bessie Cleveland

Elsa Contreras

Darryl Davis

Marcia & Pete Dowd

Cindy Fricke of Harris Bank

Tamilenn Garrett

Barbara Harris

Byron Johns

Tim Kastner

Wendell Lewis

Deborah McGee

Kristen Nickles

Michael & Tanya Pettis

Christopher Robinson

Contents

Introduction

Okay, so I am just going to be real and say that writing the introduction to this book has been the most challenging part. I mean, where do I begin? How do I begin? I can tell you, the moment I am writing these very words, I am sitting in my apartment, looking at a picture of my lovely yet, mischievous niece and I on my desk. In the kitchen awaits a slice of pizza and some fries sitting in the oven screaming "Eat me. Eat me." I must admit though, as I was walking to the pizza joint to pick up my pizza slice, fries, and a drink, I had this urgency to write the introduction to this book. While I was walking home, and the pizza was smelling extra good, I thought of almost every reason to get around doing this, but then I thought about you. Yes, you! The very person reading this right now is who I thought about. You may be thinking "Oh please! Hold off on eating a pizza slice and fries, MAN WHAT ARE YOU THINKING!!!"

The truth of the matter of is, a little over a year ago, I probably would have come home, put in my favorite action adventure DVD, then sat and enjoyed the pizza and fries without hesitation. However, since that time, so much in my life has transformed. Why? Over the past year, I have made some major choices. You see in 2005, I was working in a law firm making a good $50,000 a year in Chicago. I had my own office, a great staff to work with, great bonuses, and fringe benefits like you would not believe! Heck, for the Holidays, I would get a large tin of Carmel, Cheese, and Salted popcorn that my family and I could feast on for a whole month. Yet, even with making all that money, getting all the perks, and knowing all the people that I did, I was not happy. I was not enjoying my life fully.

Well, let me take that back, I was somewhat happy. I mean really come on! A guy like me, great job, great personality *and* great looks! What didn't I have? What was I missing? The truth … I was missing my dream, my future and ultimately … my life.

For the last few years, I have been working with teens across the country. First it started with me being a coach for the Northern Illinois Leadership Seminar. The next step for me was becoming one of the Keynote speakers for the same seminar. Did I make extra money becoming a keynote speaker? Of course not, I did a lot of volunteer speeches just to put myself out there. The most I would get is a "you were great" at the end of the day. I did this while I was working the $50K a year job, so I could still afford to buy my pizza slice and fries. However, there is something I want to share with you. The first time I did my first keynote speech, I discovered something that I knew existed. While working on that stage, I felt so comfortable. It was like being home for the first time. I had a moment where I said "I can do this every day!" Have you ever had a moment like that? I remember being on that stage doing a speech named "Don't Be Scurred!" I was talking to about 150 bright, energetic, and full of hope teens, just like you and the light bulb in my head came on! "I am experiencing my *Dream*. Now I want it to be my life!' To this very day, I still cannot put into words the magic that happened on that stage.

Though working in the field of law was wonderful, I had found a greater sense of joy and purpose in my life. For years, I knew I had a knack for helping and encouraging people. It was not odd for people to call me teacher or "Dr. Jackson." It was just something that seemed to come naturally. Standing on that stage, delivering that speech was a turning point in my life.

Well, around September of 2005, I made one of the boldest moves in my life. I chose to resign from my wonderful job at the law firm to pursue my dream full time. How was I going to do it exactly? I had no freakin' clue! My last day at the office was November 30, 2005. It was one of the hardest choices I had ever made, yet I felt okay about it.

Since I resigned I've had the honor and privilege to share my story with may across the country. What is my story? I am merely someone who made a choice to live his dream. While pursuing my dream I saw how my future fam was. "Fam" by the way is short for family and everyone that I speak to I consider family. My fam still amazes me with its strength, power, energy, zest for life, and willingness to take risks. I am amazed at the power teens have today! So many teens have gone after their dream. Many more have not. For me I see this as a problem. I firmly believe that everyone on this earth should have the right to go after their dream and fulfill what they feel their purpose in life is. Too many people, including myself at one point, just accepted "I don't have time for my dream." Or "my dream is too big, so I will never be able to fulfill it, so why try to go after it?"

Nowadays, school is so focused around SATs, ACTs, fitness test, and even prom date tests it is almost too crazy to have a conversation about dreams. This saddens me especially considering that pursuing your dream can be one of the most rewarding experiences in life. That, "fam," is why I am sitting here today typing out these words while a slice of pizza and some fries are waiting in the oven.

In my opinion, directing you to fill your life with happiness and give you some things that will help you accomplish your dream, is more important than a pizza slice and fries. You are reading this book for a reason. Whether you picked up the book because you knew me, a friend gave it to, or you liked the title and just wanted to see what it was all about, you have been chosen and given permission to live your dream.

Before I even continue further, to the Guidance Counselors out there reading this book, this is not a disregard for what you do. I know you do your jobs well. I know, you are good at what you do, and I also know that you have a great influence on many. Trust me I know. My guidance counselor was one of the greatest. Her name was Mrs. Caldwell at Bloom Township High School in Chicago Heights, Illinois. I love her and she was a great counselor. However, between scheduling my next classes and trying to figure out my next electives and when I would take the next tests, we never really had a conversation about dreams or even what dreams were, let alone pursuing them. So if nothing else, this is a supplement to the great services you currently offer and for that I thank. Thank you for being the contribution that you are to your schools.

Now back to you. This book is more so a journey than anything else. I will be sharing some great stories with you. Some of them mine, some of them my friends, and some of them family. Now, don't get it twisted, this story is not just about me, but it is about some tools to pursue your dream which in turn offers you your best life ever.

If nothing else, this book is going to give you some serious info, mad knowledge, and some crazy skills to use today and in the future. I truly believe that if you take what's offered in this book, you will see a whole new world of opportunity. And to me, that is very important. More important than a slice of pizza and some fries.

This book covers a great deal of things from You Being You to knowing There Is Always Going To Be a Hatah! I am very convinced that this book will add to your life and I'll even be bold enough to say it will transform your life.

So, while I'm about to go warm up my pizza slice and fries, you go onto Chapter 1 and let your new and true life begin!!!

1

There's Always Going To Be a "Hatah" (Hater)

You have just completed breaking the school record for the best long jump on the track team. When this feat is met by your determined spirit, you are greeted at the other end by the coach, teammates, family and friends who were there to support this very moment. Not only did you beat the State record, you also bolstered your team to first place! How sweet is that? Can I get a "SO SWEET!" (And this is where you bust out loud and say SO SWEET!)

While relishing in this accomplishment, you notice one of your teammates standing on the side giving you a half-hearted smile. When the teammate offers you a congratulatory handshake, it sucks way more than the smile. This reaction from your teammate kind of pulls you out of your euphoric state of victory. "Why are they acting like that?" you ask yourself. While taking the bus ride back to school you lean back in the uncomfortable chair with a big smile on your face recapping your victory.

While in this moment you hear someone say "I don't understand why everyone is going crazy over that jump! It wasn't like it was some life changing event! I could have beat the record with my eyes closed, hands tied behind my back and a 20 pound weight hanging around my neck."

Realizing this conversation is about you, you do what's normal … you jump up, turn around and drop kick that teammate in the mouth like Neo from the movie Matrix and shout "try doing that with your eyes closed, hands tied behind your back and a 20 pound weight around your neck!" Okay, so comeback to the real world. Of course you heard it and brushed it off your shoulder like a grain of salt. At least that is my hope.

I use this example to make a point. No matter how much of an accomplishment you make, no matter how good you are at something, or how you stand out from others … There is always going to be a hater! But guess what! After reading this chapter, it is my hope to give you the signals of someone who is a hater and avoid them becoming a part of your crew (something we will talk about later).

DEFINITION OF A HATAH

Let's define Hater or what I like to call a Hatah.

> *Hatah (hay—tah): A person who spews forth negative words and/or actions toward someone else. Actions include talking about someone in a negative way to other people or trying to do something that will purposely sabotage what another person is doing or who the other person is. The hatah's are also prone to serving "hatahrade" or always found in a state of "hatahration."*

Now this definition is not to say that these people are hateful, but it is just a word used to really show the clarity of where these people are compared to your future.

WHY THE HATAHS?

You may ask "why?" It is not the Million dollar question, but it is the running a close second on the list. In my experiences and just knowing the experiences of others, I have narrowed it down to three reasons people choose to serve up the hatahrade.

Reason # 1—Lack of Understanding

My career in high school was a little different than the norm. I was tall and because of this, everyone thought that I should have been a basketball player. However, to their dismay, I went the artistic route. One of my favorite activities was being on the speech team. I was a member of the National Forensics League better known as the NFL (LOL). The speech team had many events that anyone could participate in. In the Illinois High School arena some of the events included Dramatic Duet Acting, Humorous Duet Acting, Extemporaneous speaking, and Verse which was poetry reading. The events that I participated in were Dramatic Interpretation and Original Comedy. My strongest event was Dramatic Interpretation. The purpose of this event was for one person to act out a scene which involved two or more characters. Ummm hummm, you heard me right, one person portraying two different characters in one scene all at the same time *(stop acting like you haven't done that when no one was looking)*.

One year I performed very well in one of the tournaments and was a medal winner. Silver to be exact (I wish someone wrote this book while I was in school because after reading it, I know I would have taken the Gold at the next competition.) ANYHOO!!! By winning the silver medal, and the overall team doing well, I was recognized as one of the top performers for the school which made the headlines in the morning announcements and the school newspaper. It just so happened, that same weekend, the football team got smashed! So bad that the football team's announcement was made in 4 seconds compared to the 3 minutes the speech team got. It was like the difference in news coverage between Beyonce', and the girl who did backup dancing for her. Needless to say, the Hatah's began coming out of the woodworks. Throughout the day, I got called a lot of names like "speech freak" "drama king" "drama queen" even "fag." This name calling came only because I did well in an event that a lot of people had no clue about.

By the end of the day, I got tired of the name calling and just stopped someone who called me a name and said "What's up man? Why you gotta call me out of my name?" He snapped back and said "You get all this recognition for being on some freaking speech team doing something dramatic. No one even knows what drama interpretive is" I interrupted quickly and corrected him "Dramatic Interpretation?" "Well whatever you call it. What is that? Who ever heard of that? The football team is working their butts off and everyone knows what we do, but you Mr. Popular all of a sudden for something no one has ever heard of."

I felt my ears turning a bright red and my stomach knotted up and I almost wanted to go Matrix on this dude. But for what? He was suffering from what I like to call "Guided Ignorance" which simply means here is someone who is going with what everyone else is going on because they do not want to search out necessary information. When I think back on it, it's hilarious because this guy wasn't even a starting player on the football team. I took a deep breath and parted my lips to say "Dramatic Interpretation is when one person acts out two or more people in a dramatic scene, it has to be memorized, characters must be developed from dialogue and dialect to the physiology, oh wait you might not understand what that means, physiology means body posture and body language. And for your info, we work just as hard as the football team. We train, condition, and practice just like the football team. The only real difference is the football team wears football helmets and we wear ties. But what trips me out is we are playing for the same school. You are competing on the football field and I am competing inside a classroom at another school, but we are on the same team."

You should have seen this guys face. His eyes got big and his bottom lip dropped. Since I was on a roll I went on to say "Dude, I am sorry that the football team got creamed this weekend, but it is so unfair for you to be hating on me when you don't even understand what I do." It got real quiet. "Man I'm sorry." he said, "I didn't know." "It's cool dude, but before you drink on the hatahrade, make sure you read the label and understand the contents. It might be bad for your health."

With that example given, it is sad to say, but because a lot of people don't understand certain things, they tend to become "hatah's." The simple fact that a lot of people don't realize they are doing this makes it even worse in some cases. It ties into the old saying there is a "fear of the unknown." Instead of people looking to turn the unknown into the known, some choose to continue the journey down the Guided Ignorance path, which in fact makes the "hatah" surface. Can you think of instances like this?

Reason # 2—Jealousy

You are going to discover that there are people out there who are hatah's simply because you are being you. To be more precise, there are some people who are jealous of you. They may be jealous of your grades, how you dress, who you hang out with, what your house looks like or even the boyfriend or girlfriend that you have. What makes it worse for the hatah's, they see that you are proud of what you have. Come on, wouldn't you be proud of having straight A's or a nice car for school?

So here is where I have to make a confession about being the "hatah." I was in 8th grade. There was this dude who was not like all the other dudes. He dressed his own way, he was always clean cut and what impressed me most about this guy was he was very confident. His confidence showed in his walk, talk and even how he interacted with others. He made it seem like he was King of the World! "Who does he think he is?" I would always question. I would spend hours ticked off at this guy because he had it all together. Before I knew it, I was talking about this dude behind his back. Why? He didn't do anything wrong to me. He never said anything bad to me. He would even hang out at my table for lunch sometimes.

So one day, while in the midst of "hatin'" on him, word got around that I was talking about him. Of course you know he confronted me about it. He wasn't all in my face or anything. Truth be told, he was very laid back about it. That drove me even crazier. At least he could have been throwing books and foaming at the mouth about what he heard come from me. BUT NOOO! He had to be all calm. It would have been cool if he approached me foul and then that would have given me reason to rumble *(now for those of you who have thought that I have been Mr. Good Kid this whole time ... YEAH RIGHT!)*. He came at me very smooth and just wanted to know why I was talking about him. My immediate response was "you dress funny." Just as soon as those words crossed my lips I felt like the biggest JERK in the world!

It was like everyone who was hanging around to see what was going to happen, gave me this *"what?"* look. He laughed at me and said "if that's the only reason you don't like me man, just don't wear what I wear and you'll be cool." "DANGIT!!!" I thought to myself. I looked like a fool not only at the fault of my own mouth but also at the hands of this guy getting cool points, and from our conversation he was quickly gaining more. I stood there dumbfounded. My buddy at the time looked at me and said "man that was dumb" followed by this goofy laugh that I wish I could just capture in a bottle and throw away into the bottomless pit of nothingness.

That day it took me a little longer to get home. I was trying to figure out why I was being a hatah? Why was I hatin' on this guy from school. He was cool, didn't do anything to me, and he had almost every reason to punch me in the face. I thought "why can't I be cool like that?" Sure enough, as that thought came across my mind I realized I wanted to be like him. I wanted to be this cool kat! Then I realized, this whole time I was jealous of him.

There it was, Reason #2, jealousy. I was jealous of this guy from school all because I wanted to be cool like him. Because I wasn't, I immediately took the easy way out and started to trip about it. Here is where I offer a word of caution. Be careful. You would be amazed at how some kids want to be like you and because they are not, they play the game of "hatin" on you.

There was one thing I never stopped to think about during my time of being a hatah. I could have gotten to know this guy for who he was. I could have asked him "man how did you get to be so cool." One of the dilemmas that hatah's will find themselves in, is breaking through the fear of the unknown. To breakthrough the fear of the unknown takes some work and it even takes some guts. We can spend a lifetime of trying to look good or defend our differences in life when in fact, if we gave that up for even a moment, we open ourselves to a whole new world. If you find yourself in a situation that even sounds close to Reason #2, consider this a time of choice right now. You can remain on the path of Guided Ignorance ... or you can breakthrough and shatter the world of the unknown ... Think about it.

Reason # 3—Insecurity

There are some hatah's out there who merely hate for their lack of self-esteem. They are insecure in who they are, therefore, they try to find a way around it and front off on other people. While in school trying to fit into the "in-crowd" proves challenging for a large number of students, whether they will admit it or not. Look at it from your standpoint. Have you ever tried to fit into the in-crowd, but didn't have what it takes? You either didn't dress like everyone else, you didn't have "the look," or maybe you didn't have the "financial status." During any of those times, did you question who you were and if you were good enough? If so, that is exactly what I mean by insecurity. Your self-esteem has been threatened.

This is Reason # 3 because there are those who stay in that moment of not feeling like they are "enough" and the hatahration begins right there. Because the threat is present of not being enough, the hatah in someone will surface and surface strong. So how does the insecurity show without someone coming right out and saying "I'm Insecure?"

Have you ever been around someone who was constantly saying, "Well I can sing better than you, you can't dance like me, I will beat you in that game any time" or the famous line "you're cute … just not cute like me, but you're okay."

Those who suffer from this reason can be one of the trickiest to figure out. On the surface, you will almost fall for the whole "I am better than you" act, but after while it begins to eat away at you. You have to be careful. This reason usually surfaces in those who are closest to us. The ones we hang out with. The one's who we sometimes call our friends.

It is also tricky because it is very close to reason #2 which is Jealousy. The reason it is tricky because who wants to really think or even accept that someone that close to them would be jealous. You would almost want them to be proud of you and your accomplishments.

When you have friends like this, their insecurity will begin to setup a level of insecurity in you. You will begin to question if you are good enough. If you can do something better. If you are cute enough. Before you know it, you almost find yourself running to them for constant approval and validation. This is when the insecurity has surfaced in you. It is then when they will pick on your insecurities to hide their own. Why would they spend time on their insecurities when in fact the both of you spend time on yours?

Let's look at an example. You and your friend are in the same event. You win the event, and your friend comes in 4th place. Instead of getting the "great job, you did really good," what you will hear is "today was an off day for me. I couldn't have won anyway. Oh! Congratulations by the way." HELLO!!! What type of congratulations is that? Before you know it, you are questioning if you won by fluke.

Be very careful of those who fall under this reason. Think about it. Could you be around someone or even call someone your friend if they are constantly reminding you of what you lack? There are so many other people in the world that would cherish your friendship.

However, before you write off a friend because you feel there is an issue of insecurity, really get in their world. How are things going at home for them? How are things going in school? What are their grades like? How is their relationship with their girlfriend or boy-friend? Has something happened in their life recently that could have a tremendous affect on their everyday life? Have they recently loss a family member or friend? Have they recently come out of the closet? I am asking you to get into their world, because sometimes "Life Happens."

I am quite sure that in choosing your friends or associates, you did not go out saying "ok I am looking for a friend who belittles me and makes me feel like crap." If you did, I am going to ask that you skip a few chapters and read "Who's got your back." You may need a little assistance in the friend picking area.

With that being said, usually the insecurity does not show right away. One thing you will notice about the pattern of being a hatah, it is 99% triggered by something or someone else. When it comes to insecurity, often times, it can be triggered by something at home or even at school. Here is where I reach out to you as a friend who believes they may have a friend suffering from this. Often times becoming a hatah all of a sudden can be a symptom of something that is going on deeper. Did you know that one of the reasons teenagers go into depression is because their parents may have divorced recently? Did you know that those who come out to friends, usually do not come out to parents because they are afraid they may not be wanted by their parents afterward? Then there are those cases that the parent finds out and then they are made to feel worthless or insignificant in some instances.

I bring all this up to say that the hatahrade being served by your friend may be their way of trying to make themselves feel worthy when they have in other cases been made to feel unworthy. So if you have a friend who seems to have taken a sip of the hatahrade recently, look to see if there is more to the story than they are telling you.

Now, you do not have to go out and get a detective badge and act like you are on Law & Order. Sometimes, all you have to do is ask. If they do not give you the heads up or share with you and you see some things that may concern you, seek help or advice. If you are in school, speak with a trusted teacher, counselor, or even dean. Or you can look to those in your community.

So to give you a heads up, being a hatah is not always voluntary, but it will have some of the same affects as if it were. Just know that when it is involuntary, you can step in and pull that person out of the state of hatahration. You got that? Cool. So to recap, the three main reasons people can become Hatah's are:

Reason # 1—Lack of Understanding

Reason # 2—Jealousy

Reason # 3—Insecurity

With these as guiding lights of what to look out for in other people, assure yourself you don't fall into one of these categories. Sometimes, you have to take a very strong look at yourself. Are you always jumping to a conclusion with a friend even when you don't understand all the facts? Have you given your friend grief because you feel they dress better or get better grades? Do you feel you are not good enough, but you always tend to find that your friend is worse off than you? Do you find yourself constantly giving advice, but turning it down when others are sharing with you?

If you feel you are a little bit too familiar with these situations … Time to take a check-up from the neck up because you could run a high risk of being a hatah yourself. Let's be frank, this topic may almost be a bit uncomfortable for you, but realize that when you learn better you *are* better. It is almost like diving into a 2 foot deep pool head first. After you do it the first time, you realize that you should not dive into shallow waters or you just might break your neck.

Another reason this topic may be a bit uncomfortable is because it is so close to the word Hate. Some of you may even be thinking "why is he using such a harsh word?" For some of you it may be making you take a closer look at who you call your friends, associates and even yourself.

At first, I thought "hatah's, what a harsh word to use." I mean when we think of haters we think of the obvious reasons for hate. Whether it be hate crimes due to religion, race, sexuality, or even choice, it still stands out as an extreme notion. However in my life, as time progressed and experiences seemed to riddle my life, I started to realize that there are going to be people who will purposely try to sabotage your life! Yes! You will share some things with them that you want to accomplish and they will try to drag it down. In my book, that sucks. I mean who wants a friend like that?

Maybe *they* think it is a stupid idea. Maybe *they* feel you don't have enough talent to get what you want. Or maybe, just maybe, *they* feel that what you want is too hard to get and they don't want to see you get hurt. And then there are those who just don't want you to have it at all! Hatahs! Do you get where I am coming from?

This chapter is not about putting people in your life on front street, but it is more about giving you the tools you need to know to recognize them. Being in school can be a time where it may seem like you are running across Hatahs everyday. Instead of looking at this in a negative way, after you are done with this chapter, you will view it in a different light. NO.... Hatah's are not a positive thing, but knowing who is and what to do with them *without drop kicking them* is!!!

Now you may be saying to yourself "I get it A'ric, I know what a hatah is, I know how to recognize a hatah, now how do I get around this?" Glad you asked. Let's go to the next chapter, and the answer is …

2

YBY!!!! (You Be You)

This is one of the most important tools. You be you! I have had plenty of people come up to me from students to parents, complain to me about the hatah's. Then the immediate question that follows is "what do I do?" My response is "There is one person on the face of this earth that you wake up to every morning, go to sleep with every night and are with every moment of the day. That person is you. My suggestion is talk to that person in private and find out what is the best solution for you." I am always given this dumbfounded *"yeah right"* look.

When you are under the rule of your parents, it is easier said than done. And having your parents, teachers and other people who feel that they have a say so in your life breathing down your back, it can be very hard to find that person called "self." Well guess what ... Been there; done that; *and* got the T-Shirt.

One of the reasons Hatah's have this beef with you can be due to the fact you are living your life the way you want. Even if you are not living it 100% the way you want, to even be living 50% of it can be baffling for some. *By the way, it doesn't count if you feel you are not living 50% of your life because you are not dating Chris Brown or Kelly Clarkson! It's ok! You will find your own Chris or Kelly one day soon!*

Despite the hatah's "You Being You" can be one of the most rewarding factors in your life. It can also be that remedy for Hatah's not getting to you the way they currently do. Can you imagine living a life that is fully self-expressed? Can you imagine a life that was created and designed by you … AND IT'S HOT!!! Can you imagine doing everything the way you want and people in your life such as your parents, friends, and even teachers love it? Can you? So if you can, my question is, why just imagine it? Why not have it? Why not live and breathe it?

I am so laughing right now because I know you have come up with almost every excuse why you are not having this life called "Your Life." As I am typing this I am literally laughing because I have heard just about all of them. "My parents won't let me." "I don't have time to be myself." "I don't know who I want to be." "No one will like me if I be myself." "My dog ate my image." There are so many excuses to name. The most popular one I have heard is "How can I learn to be myself?" If that is one of your questions, I can answer that one for you.

I have come with the five steps to being yourself. They have proven to allow me to be myself and love myself over and over again, not to mention the students and even adults who I have shared these five steps with. But before we go there, I must warn you. You must be you because you *want* to be you. Don't choose to be you because you got a hatah that is getting on your nerve. Being you should be a choice and not a "have to." You should choose to do this for you and no one else. When you do, not being bothered by hatah's is merely a small bonus. What you accomplish is living your life and loving the life you live. I can explain better by a personal example.

While in high school, I was as skinny as a toothpick. My grandmother would always make fun of me and say "boy you so skinny I almost don't see you when you turn to the side." However, when I graduated from high school, less than a year later I moved into my own place. The joy of this? I LEARNED TO COOK!!! That meant I could eat anything I wanted to eat. I could eat when I wanted to eat. Vegetables? Who had time to prep veggies when I could have pork chops, hamburgers, hot dogs, and pizza whenever I wanted? Let's not even talk about the Cookies & Cream Ice Cream.

Needless to say, within a year's time, I picked up almost 40 additional pounds. By this time, my grandmother would see me and say "ya kind of filling out your britches aren't cha?" I would laugh but I knew she was telling the truth. I went from a 32 waist to a 38, almost 40. Close your mouth! I know it's shocking.

So a year later I would be watching TV with my "boo" and would constantly hear about how sexy Will Smith was or how some of the actors on TV were gorgeous and had gorgeous bodies. I didn't know then, but I knew I was being a hatah to the 100th power to these people on TV who didn't even know me! So one day, I said I was going to the gym to get a body like one of the dude's on TV. If I did this, then my "boo" would be all over me. Of course I was acting like I could go to the gym and say "can I have a body like Omarion for $500, thanks." Very naïve on my part right?

So I enrolled in the gym. In three months, I went to the gym ummm, about 4 times. But of course I would still hear the "you would look so good with a body like that" story over and over again. So I decided to take it seriously and go the gym hard core. After about a year later, I was in the gym at least twice a week. Not enough to have HUGE results, but enough to show my effort of going to the gym. My "boo" really liked the results. That made me happy. However, what I noticed was whenever we had a disagreement, or we were not on good terms, I would purposely not go to the gym as a form of punishment. Eventually, we broke up. After the break up, I didn't care about the gym, and underneath it all, I didn't care about myself anymore. "No one wants to get with me" would be my constant thought.

I got use to beating myself up until, my health was going down the drain big time *and* I was back up to my original size. The following year was all about blaming my breakup for my current body. When that didn't work, I began to blame me being too busy at work. MY LIFE WAS ONE BIG EXCUSE!!!!

To make my life better, I chose to enter this 12 week fitness challenge. I would get all the food, vitamins, even the nice work out gear and try this challenge. I started the challenge a good 5 times, yet, I never finished it. The furthest I got into the challenge was up to 4 weeks. Of course I had the greatest excuses in the book. I mean I should have written a book on excuses because they were awesome.

One day, I was talking to my sister. My sister is my best friend and we have been through a lot together. She is my ace! So while I was talking to her, I told her, "yeah, I'm about to do that 12 week challenge again." Now, I have to note here that every time I started this challenge, she was my number one cheerleader. However, this particular day, when I told her, the response was not "good." The response was "are you going to finish it this time?" To this day, my sister has not said anything so piercing. She called my bluff. She knew all of the excuses, therefore she was not really interested anymore. Did I go to the gym the next week? OF COURSE NOT!!

However, what did happen, that conversation with my sister triggered something deep within. Why had I been trying to get this "perfect body?" Why was I on a mission? Why would I go on the mission and never complete it? One day out of the blue the answer came plain as day. I had been doing these challenges to prove something to someone else ... I never did them for ME. The main ingredient to this accomplishment was missing ... ME. At that time, I found reasons for why I wanted to do it for myself. A week later, I took to the gym like a fish to water. Despite the soreness and sometimes strict eating habits, I was loving every moment of it because this was something I wanted to do. 12 weeks later, there I was in the gym taking my after photos to show the accomplishment of completing the challenge. What was so amazing about that day, my sister was there for the photo shoot. She cried when she saw me taking the pictures. She later asked "what was different this time." I told her that instead of doing it for someone else, I did it for myself. A few weeks later, inspired by me, my sister took the challenge. Now that is the type of life I love to live.

My reason for sharing this story is to show you that when you choose for any other reason other than yourself, you run the risk of not accomplishing what you set out to do. This is a warning. If you choose to *Be You*, choose because this is what *you* want. Not what your parents, teachers, brothers, sisters, boyfriend, or girlfriend wants. If you choose for a reason outside of you, it will be easy to give up what you desire. You clear on that?

So now that we know you want to do this, let's look at the 5 steps.

STEP # 1—BE REAL WITH YOURSELF

When someone meets you for the first time, do they really meet you? Or do they meet someone who you think they will like? Heads up, step #1 is the hardest. However, if you take this one, and you begin mastering this, you have laid a solid foundation to *You Being You.*

What do you like? Why do you like what you like? What type of music do you like? Why? What type of clothes do you like to wear? Why? What's your favorite movie genre? Why? Are some of these questions a bit difficult to answer? Or is the "why" following the question more difficult? In chapter 1 I spoke about trying to be with the "In-Crowd." The common thought in school is if you are not part of a group or usually by yourself, you are categorized as being weird or strange. To avoid this feeling or label, many students will get in where they can fit in. This is not a bad thing. However, what begins to happen in some cases, the person takes on the likes and dislikes of the overall group and overlooks what they themselves like and dislike. If the group dresses a certain way, you may feel it is important to dress the same, or you run the risk of not being in the group any longer.

So now's the time to ask yourself, are you being real with yourself? Do you like everything that the group does? Do you like everything they wear? Do you like all the places they hang out? If the answer is no, then why are you doing them? Only you can answer that, but again are you being real with yourself?

Step #1 is not about getting rid of who you are hanging out with or what you wear, but it is about taking a look at yourself. So if you answered one of the "why" questions by saying "because the group I hang out with does it to," guess what, you are well on your way to being real with yourself.

Being real with yourself may sound really hard. It's not that it is hard, but it takes work to get to being real with yourself. What do you need to do to be real with yourself? The answer? Just be aware. When you are doing something, ask yourself if you are doing this because you want to. If you don't want to do it, why are you doing it? Do you choose not to do it? We are taught to go along with the group's choice, but the real question is, where is that written in stone? If there is something you like, like it because it's what you like. And if it is something that you don't like, but you know you are doing it because you want to be a part of the group, then be real with yourself and admit that for what it is. You can easily say, you don't like going to the mall to hang out, but you do it to hang with your friends. Do you see the distinction?

Being real with yourself is merely stating what is real for you. Now, don't be a con. A con is one who forces themselves to believe they like something or want to do something overlooking their true feelings. It is almost like saying I love the mall because I love going to the mall with my friends, when deep down, you know, you hate the mall. This is where you are not being real with yourself.

When you are able to stop and be real about it all, you are laying a strong foundation for *You Being You*. This is not about separating yourself from others because of a difference of likes and dislikes. *You being You* is about knowing you enough to know the likes and dislikes and still be able to have your friends or hang with a certain group.

Being real with yourself is all about being aware and present to what you are doing and what you are choosing to do. Will there be conflicts every once in a while? HECKY YEAH!!! But when it all boils down to it, in order to live a life where you are you, you have to know the real you. Be real enough to accept the good, the bad, and even the stupid about yourself. If your grades suck, be real with yourself and realize that you may not be studying the way you should. Or maybe you are not doing your homework. Maybe you are ditching class. So being real with yourself would be acknowledging that these could be the reasons why your grades suck. Not being real with yourself would be knowing that you don't do your work but you are saying your teacher is not a good teacher, that's why your grades are not good. Or, you don't have enough time to study. Or even none of the teachers like me. GET OVER IT!

Is being real with yourself going to be one of the greatest moments of your life? Probably not, but when you do this work, you are setting yourself apart from those who are cons. It is so much easier to not be real with yourself and just make things up as you go along. But where does that leave you at the end of the day? Look at it this way, if you are so busy trying to be someone else, you cheat yourself and your life. You cheat by not letting the world see you. Better yet, let's look at it this way, if you are cheating yourself, YOU will never see the true you and what your greatness is. You are so worth it. So with that in mind, when you put in the work to be real with yourself, you are preparing yourself for a life of clarity and success beyond your imagination. You will have been so successful with your life that NO ONE could tell you anything different. At least they couldn't tell you anything you already didn't know. Not even that crazy voice residing inside of your head which leads me to Step # 2.

STEP # 2—SEPARATE YOU FROM THE VOICE IN YOUR HEAD

Now before you think I am going off the deep end, I have to let you know that all of us have a voice in our head. Okay, to prove it, I have a test for you to take. You are going to put your finger on this page to bookmark where you are and you are going to take about 15 seconds and sit still and not say anything. You ready and go …

Okay. During the 15 seconds, did you hear that little voice? Yes? If you did what was it saying to you? Now if the answer was no, did you put the book down and hear things like "I'm not gonna take this test." "What voice is he talking about, I don't hear a voice." "Is my time over yet?" "What time is dinner?" Well my friend if you can recall anything like that, say hello to your little friend "the voice."

No! You are not crazy and you are not alone. 99.99999% of the human beings on this earth have that voice. It's not a good or a bad thing. It just is what it is. Now can we turn this voice off? YEAH RIGHT! Of course not! It is going to be there until the end of time my friend.

With that in mind, let's talk about Step #2. You are to separate "you" from the voice in your head. Now having this voice can be helpful in some cases and then at times it can be somewhat disheartening. The "voice" or what we call the consciousness can be a great tool in many cases. That voice can help you make some choices, see some things from a different perspective, and can even be a great ally to *You being You.* So why separate *You* from the voice in your head?

Have you ever had moments in your life where you have done something and it didn't work out for whatever reason, then all of sudden that voice says "YOU STUPID!!!" This is a reaction, and as powerful as your voice can be proactively, it can be as powerful when it is reacting. The "YOU STUPID" comment heard in your head was a reaction to a situation. What happens right at that point for some, is they take statement literally. All of sudden because the voice in your head has stated this, you make that mean that you are literally stupid. What is the long term result? Whenever a situation like this arises again, you avoid it or you overlook it. Why? Because you feel you're "stupid."

Let's look at an example of this. There is someone who you are really attracted to. You think they are so HOT! You know that they would be the greatest asset to your upcoming Prom pictures. In order to make that happen, you have to ask this person to prom. You get dressed for the day of the official ask, you looking good, smelling good, I mean you looking so tasty that you want to ask yourself out to prom! You been practicing your walk, your wink of the eye as you walk down the hallway, you even know where and how you are going to sit right before you pop the question. That time comes. You are confident. You got it all together; you sit down you pop the question with smoothness like never before. The response? They laugh in your face and say "no, sorry, I don't think so." You try to play it off so you don't lose cool points, then as you get up to walk away gracefully that voice in your head says "that was dumb! You're dumb!" You get upset storm out of the cafeteria, run to the bathroom, hide in stall and pretend like you are not hurt as you drown yourself in your own tears. (I know that's a little extreme, but just thought it sounded good.) So sitting there keeping you company during this tumultuous time is your little friend "the voice." Telling you how dumb you are to have even asked, you are not good enough for that to be your prom date, and a whole bunch of other B.S. that goes along with it. (Can you tell this is a personal experience?)

From that day forward, that little voice runs your life when it comes to taking chances and taking risks. Whenever you prepare yourself for something big, you don't follow through because you think "you're dumb" and it's not going to work. You constantly tell yourself you are not good enough over and over and over again until what you were good in doing, you don't do good anymore. And who's there the whole time? That little voice reassuring you of it all.

So, here is where it all ends. You are not that voice in your head! Give it up. Repeat after me "I AM NOT THE VOICE IN MY HEAD!" Yes, we all do stupid stuff but that does not mean that we are stupid. Your conscience is a powerful tool. You can use your conscience to create greatness, or your conscience can use you for self destruction. One disease that is really strong in high school now is depression. I know I am being bold in saying this, but I am confident enough to say to you ... Show me someone who is depressed, and I can show you someone who is listening to that voice in their head 24/7.

Step # 2 is about not falling for that. The voice is just a voice. The voice is not waking you up in the morning, putting you in the shower and getting you dressed for school. Look at it this way. That little voice is your 24 hour 7 day a week personal radio station, giving moment by moment commentary. That's cool right? I mean really, if you think about it, you have a radio station dedicated completely to you. With that in mind, you must treat it like a radio station. Follow me on this one. What's your favorite radio station? Okay, now that you know that, do you like *everything* that radio station plays? Do you like *all* the artist? Do you listen to *all* of the artist, or do you change the station every once in awhile? Do you believe *everything* that radio station says on its news portion? ALL OF IT?

Now that we know what works and does not work for you and your favorite radio station, let's apply that to your personal 24/7 radio station named WK_____ (Insert your name in the blank.) Just like a radio station, you don't have to like every thing you hear on your personal station. You don't have to believe *every* thing this radio station plays. The only thing that really sucks about your radio station is that it is on 24/7. As much as you want to turn it off or shut it up, it will always be there … playing in the background … like elevator music.

There is a wonderful thing about this though. You can control your station and even fine tune your station. When ever your voice says to you "YOU SUCK" just simply take a moment and say to you voice "thanks for sharing, have a nice day." I am so serious. I have an assignment for you. For the next day, tune into your radio station. Listen closely and I guarantee you that the little voice is going to have some unfavorable comment to share with you. When it does share, say "thanks for sharing" and move on. What you are doing is fine tuning your station. There will come a point and time where your voice will say what it says but it won't be as loud because you know YOU ARE NOT YOUR VOICE!

The flip end of that, know that your voice is going to say things like "You are so Great" "You are fabulous" "You are off the CHAIN!!" Here is where you can reinforce that by saying "thanks, I know, glad you recognized." Okay, so your response may not be that flavored, but realize you have the power to empower that voice. Now, do not confuse your voice. What do I mean by that? When that little voice says "You did great on that" don't confuse it by saying "no I didn't, I sucked." DING DING DING!!! If you say that, you are giving that little voice permission to run the "You suck" commercials and the "Feel sorry for me" songs to run on your radio station all day long.

It is like downloading music on your IPod. You choose what you want to go on there. One day you may love what you have on there. A week later you may want to either update or change the music, but you are free to do so. You are not stuck with it. If you choose to keep music on there that you don't like, that is on you. That was your choice. That is just like your WK _____ (Insert your name in the blank again) radio station. You program it. It takes time. Just know that as much as you program it, you will always hear that voice say things that you don't care for. I can guarantee you from the most famous athlete, to the most famous attorney; from the most successful Actor/Actress to the most successful Brain Surgeon, they too hear that voice. They all have their own radio station. What's the difference? They are fine tuning their station from moment to moment. Just know that you are not that little voice in your head.

STEP # 3—MAKE CHOICES

You are at the mid point of *You Being You*. It is some work, yet this next step can be extremely fun and challenging. Making choices for yourself and your life is so under-rated. For some time I would wonder why are we quick to allow others to make choices for us. It ranges from the people that we hang out with, to those who we have as our mentors or even friends. We are so quick to involve them in making choices for us. Then in some cases, we even give up our choice making power to someone else and let them make the choice for us.

I speak from experience. I am ... no let me take that back, I was one of those people who I like to call "choice seekers." What is a Choice Seeker? Someone who finds people to be their associate, friend, colleague, and in some cases, boyfriend or girlfriend, who they know will be more than happy to help you make your choices. So what I would do is seek out these people. Usually, I would feel that they were smarter than me or had a lot going for themselves. I would allow them into my life and even allow them to see what my life was like. Then the time would come for me to make a choice. So what would I do? Yep, I would call that person or have a conversation with that person and share with them the choice I would have to make. I would let them know the pros and cons of the matter. After doing that, I would then ask "so if you were in my shoes what would you do?" I would sit back and listen to their response. After hearing the response, I would then say, "That's great. I think I am going to go that route."

Ultimately, I never made the choice on my own. I allowed others to make the choice for me. Sounds really powerful doesn't it? I thought I had it all figured out. I had the process down to a science. Then, after sometime I saw the backfire it would have. What would happen often was, if the choice didn't work for me, I would get upset and angry that the wrong choice was made. Then came the time when I would be the biggest jerk. I would let the person know in a very sly way that the "advice" they gave me was faulty. Then I would try to make them feel bad for giving me that advice (*I told you I was not always a saint*).

After seeing this happen over and over again and even losing some great friendships over it, I really had to examine what was I doing? Why would I always feel so incomplete? Even when the "advice" that was given was great and it worked for me, I still felt … I don't know … icky, nasty … the feeling just sucked.

Then it hit me. I was left feeling incomplete because I could not take credit for any of the choices. So I took some time and went through Step # 1 (Got real with myself) and realized that I had no right to be proud of the choices that were made because they were not *my* choices. I was a con artist. I fooled myself into believing that all the choices that I was making were mine. I was so blinded, that I had to discover I had been doing this for too long. I will admit that it hurt to come to that conclusion. I felt like crap! I even had a period after that realization where I didn't want to make any choices. I became very wishy washy. No one could depend on me. I became a flake. I would not make choices, I would not help others make choices, I just stopped making choices because I was afraid of making the wrong choice.

Continuing through Step # 1, I came to another conclusion. Me not making a choice *was* a choice. To run away from something and not make a choice or do anything about it, was ultimately making a choice of not doing anything about. I was up against this dang on choice wall and it was getting on my freakin' nerves. There was no way around it. It was choose or CHOOSE. So in looking at this straight, I realized that I had to stop whining and start making choices. Within a years time of taking this on, I saw how my life began to shift because of the choices I made. I saw that my stress level was coming down. I wasn't as nasty or feisty. My days even seemed lighter and brighter. It finally dawned on me that my life was shifting because I was making choices. Not my friends, colleagues, or even the voice in my head … I was making the choices. I was calling the shots. What became clear to me is my life was mine because of my choices. Feel me? Every day, I had a choice. And everyday, I made choices.

When *you* make choices in your life, there is a level of freedom behind it all. Were all of the choices I made good? HECK NO! Some of them sucked so bad, all I could do was laugh and say "well that was my choice." But again it was *my* choice. Hear me loud and clear when I say this. There is nothing like making choices for yourself and your life. Whether good, bad, ugly, or indifferent, the mere fact that you made the choice, is freedom alone. If you choose to make the Dean's List or the Honor Roll, that is your choice. If you choose to start a Blog about the unfairness of not being able to use IPod's in the cafeteria at school, that is your choice. If you choose to skip class, that is your choice. Even if you choose to engage in risky activities such as drugs, violence or even risky sexual activity … THAT IS YOUR CHOICE! Now let me be clear about that last line. I don't agree with any of those choices, but here's the thing YOU must realize. If you engage in any of this, **you dare not say it was because someone made you do it!** Now, here is where I get a little personal. I am so sick of what I call the "they made me do it" syndrome. That is such a cop out! GET OVER IT!!!! When you do drugs, have unprotected sex, or even bully or beat someone else up, THAT IS ON YOU!!!

Imagine a life of making choices. I am not saying imagine a life of making good choices. Just imagine making choices period. I say this step is fun because everyday and almost every moment, you get to make a choice. The challenge of it all is knowing what your choice will be. Life will not be cookie cutter easy. If you think that, well, that's your choice to think that. Live a life that you choose. You have that much power in this world. How do you demonstrate that power? It is not by making choices for others, but making choices for yourself. You would be surprised at how many people live a life of not choosing, but in order for *you* to *be you*, you must make your own choices. Which leads us to Step # 4.

STEP # 4—TAKE RESPONSIBILITY

Okay, so I thought I was done talking about the whole violence, drugs, and risky behaviors, but I think this is a great way begin the conversation of taking responsibility. Let's take a look at violence. So you choose to be a bully. You wake up one morning and choose to be the kid in school that everyone is scared of, turns their allowance into every Friday, and punish those who don't and challenge any who question what you do. Got that? Okay, cool, so one day, there is a guy who doesn't turn in his allowance money to you. You send out a notice that after school, he should be ready to rumble. It's 3:30, you find him, you pulverize him, and let him know who's in charge YOU BULLY YOU!!!

The next day in school, you find out that he was sent to the hospital after your meeting, and he is currently in intensive care. What you don't know is that he has a family of bullies who are a bit tougher than you and they got the word that you were the cause of this. After school, on your way home, out of the blue there is a group of guys who pull up in a car and some of the guys get out and begin chasing you. Before you can reach home or even pick up your cell phone to call any of your "boys" they catch you. They begin to attempt to pulverize you in the fashion you delivered just the day before. A few minutes later, they have gone beyond what you did yesterday and next thing you know you are being held in an alley by some of the guys while one pulls out a knife from no where. He walks up to you and says some words that you can't quite hear because you are trying to remain conscious as you are staring at the shiny blade. Next thing you know, you feel a sharp pain shoot from your stomach as you collapse. You have been stabbed. PAUSE. Do you take responsibility? You are lying there in pain losing consciousness, do you take responsibility?

For those of you reading this, would you take responsibility? Yes? So you take responsibility for lying there bleeding because you know you brought this upon yourself? No? So you don't take responsibility because you were not trying to put the boy in the hospital before, you were just trying to show him a lesson and prove a point to everyone else.

Harsh? I know. That was intentional. What is really sad? Occurrences like this are not far fetched. As a matter of fact, for some of you reading this, this may hit too close to home. There are bullies, and even "Mean Girls" in every school. So I have one question for you. Do you understand that every choice you make, you have an impact on the world? Literally, you do. You don't impact just the people around you, in your school or even state, you impact the world. Not just today, even the future. You have that much power. So what does this have to do with taking responsibility? Everything!

When you go through step #3 you almost have to immediately jump to step # 4. In some cases you have to look at taking responsibility and incorporate that into making a choice. Taking responsibility in this context is about standing behind the choices that you have made. To stand behind your choice is a level of responsibility that many do not even consider. If we as human beings looked at what we choose to take responsibility for through our choices, the world would not be in the state that it is today. More than half of the crime would not be. Now grant it, that is a great consideration, but I am bold enough to put it out there. Maybe if they read this book first ... (wink).

To take responsibility or stand by the choice you made, you are setting yourself apart from the typical view of those who just make a choice and sit back and wait to see what happens. So what I would like for you to consider with this step, is visit this step immediately after Step #3. As a matter of fact, this step can go hand in hand with Step # 3.

Now, your choice and the outcome thereof may not always be the easiest to take responsibility for. Take a look at some of the choices you have made. Have you taken responsibility for them? Let's say you make a choice to start a food drive for a homeless shelter in your neighborhood. Take responsibility for it. That means own up to it. Stand strong in it being known that this was a choice that you made to help those in your neighborhood. "Why?" you may ask. The choice you make impacts the world. There may be others around you who have wanted to do something similar to what you have done. So when they see that you have done it AND you take responsibility for it, you give them the desire and even permission to make their choice.

How many times have you done something and your friends told you they were inspired by you, or they wanted to do something like you? That means that you have taken responsibility. A personal example for me is whenever I speak at a school or event, I choose to deliver a powerful and an impacting speech. In order to do that, I must do my work, my research and preparation. Once I have done that, I make the choice to do this and I accept the responsibility for the outcome. Some of the outcomes have been some students sharing with me some breakthroughs that they have had after hearing me speak. Whether the breakthroughs be regarding their parents getting a divorce or even being with a a family member who has cancer. Then there are even some who come out about their sexuality and who they feel they are. If I did not take responsibility for this, I would downplay it all and give the whole "oh I didn't do anything" speech.

Whenever you make a choice; whatever choice you make ... take responsibility for it. If you practice this and get into the flow of doing this often, you will see your world transform. It creates a powerful place for you to stand. To take responsibility is to embrace your choice and the results thereof. Last but not least, the final step in *You Being You* is

STEP # 5—STOP TRYING AND START BE-ING

"I'm trying my best, but it's not working" "I am trying to stay ahead of the game" "I am trying to get it." Do statements like this sound familiar? Have you ever stopped to really listen to people when they are talking? One word that is chronically used is the word "trying." One thing my colleagues, friends, and family can tell you about me, I listen closely to them and how they speak. Know this, you are what you speak. If you say you are tired, more than likely your actions are showing that. If you say you are excited, it is almost expected to see a glow about yourself and you are very animated. Look at it this way, if you say you are depressed or sad, seeing you jump around like a cheerleader and showing a great deal of energy doesn't fit does it? So now that we are clear about "we are what we speak" listen to this ... If you are trying *you* are not doing it. Again, if you are trying that means you are not doing it.

I oversee a training program for a Not-For-Profit Production Company. They are known for their Dance Theater. We meet often with the dancers to see what their process has been in the studio, how things are working, what's good, what's bad, and what's ugly. In one particular meeting, there was a dancer who was stating some things and she kept saying "I've been trying" and "I am trying." Of course my keen ear red alert went off. One of the reasons she was having some issues was because she was "trying." I brought that to her attention. Needless to say, it was not popular when I did. Even the rest of the team in the room backed off when I said "I want you to notice that you keep saying you are trying." She wasn't too thrilled about what I said and even said "I didn't say I was trying." I made a rebuttal and told her she said it constantly. For me it was hard because I knew this was not going to be an easy conversation. I asked her to take the 24 hour test and just listen not only to her voice but what she spoke. I even encouraged her to listen to herself for the next three days.

We didn't talk much after that, I knew I kind of ticked her off, but if me ticking her off was to cause her to be the great dancer that she is, I was willing to take that chance. About a month later, we had an open group discussion. In that meeting she stated "I took into consideration what A'ric said about listening to what I say and I did realize I say 'try' a lot." I'll admit, it almost brought tears to my eyes. It brought tears because a few days after our first meeting, I began to see her growth.

Step #5 is all about who you are being? You do understand that we are called "Human Beings." When you look at the word Being, it is a verb, an action. To break it down further who are you BE-ing? Now, it's not as deep as it sounds. As a matter of fact, it is just adding some stock to what William Shakespeare says "To Be or Not To Be, that is the question." I'll put it to you this way, are you trying to be an Honor Roll Student or are you BE-ing an Honor Roll Student? WAIT A MINUTE!!!! I hear you saying "well I am not an honor roll student because my grades don't show it, so how can I be an honor roll student?" Glad you asked.

Getting on the Honor Roll is a mere result of BE-ing an honor roll student. What does that mean? In order to be on the honor roll there are certain ways that you have to be to make it there. You must BE focused on your study. You must BE consistent with your work. You must BE willing to do whatever it takes to become an honor roll student. Now, let's put it in the context of trying. If you are TRYING to be focused on your study, TRYING to be consistent with your work, TRYING to be willing, THEN YOU ARE NOT BE-ING an honor roll student. Do you get the difference?

In one case you are "trying to be." If you are trying to be it means you not doing what it take to get there. That is like someone saying I am "trying" to be a millionaire. THAT SUCKS! Why? Because they are not and if they keep saying that, they are going to constantly remind themselves that they are trying Now here's the difference. When you are BE-ing an honor roll student, you are already doing, not trying to do, but doing what it takes to be an honor roll student. Same with BE-ing a Millionaire. You are doing what it takes to obtain that status. When you are BE-ing you are in action, you are doing.

Oftentimes, people look at where you are currently and quickly say that you are trying. However, when you know you are taking the actions to BE-ing someone or something, you are living a life of actively pursuing it. We have been so conditioned to look at things in this order:

If I Have It—I will Be It.

Let's use the Millionaire example.

If I have a million dollars—I will be a Millionaire.

Doesn't seem so bad does it? But here is my issue with that order. Before you can even consider yourself a millionaire, you have to have it, *then* you can be it. What if the order was this

If I Be It—I will Do It—Which Means I will Have It.

I know, it seems a little bit awkward, and that's fine. But let's apply the same Millionaire example to this order:

If I Be (or am BE-ing) a Millionaire, I will Do what Millionaires Do—Which means I will Have the money. See the difference. There is action to this one. The previous example is putting things in a past tense. Which can easily let you not take any action, and when you don't take action, you get stuck and typically don't make any changes.

When you embark upon anything new, whether it is being on the honor roll, making the track team, even choosing your career, you have to stand from a place of BE-ing. When you stand from that point, you know what it is going to take for you to have what it is that you want. If we use the conditioned order, you will always be on a hamster wheel trying to *have* something in order to *be* something. I mean, what if you don't make the honor roll. It will take back to "trying" to be on the honor roll. But, when you stand and say "I am an Honor Roll Student." What begins to happen is you make choices that support who you are BE-ing. If BE-ing an honor student is your choice, then you will know that skipping classes, or doing drugs, or not turning in homework, will have a tremendous affect on BE-ing an honor roll student. Therefore in your doing, this will almost be a threat to you having the Honor Roll Status.

To live your life in action choosing to BE instead of trying to be, this is going to inform your life and fuel your choices in a way that you have never seen before. OKAY! Test time. Over the next day, I want you to choose a way of BE-ing. Let's say you wake up tomorrow morning and say "I am BE-ing Fun today!" From that point, everything thing that you do, every choice that you make, it will be informed by you BE-ing fun. You may crack jokes like never before, you make even act goofy for your little brother of sister, but the fact is you are going to BE fun!

Now, I understand this concept may be a little difficult to grasp at first. Trust, it took me a minute to get. However, take the test and see what that does for you. I wake up every morning and say things like "I am Be-ing Loving today." "I am Be-ing Focused today." I am Be-ing a person who makes a difference in the world." Having done that in my life, has yielded some tremendous results. And guess what, you are holding one of those results in your hand right now. So STOP TRYING and START BE-ING.

There you have it! The 5 steps to you being you. Let's recap:

Step #1—Be Real With Yourself

Step #2—Separate you from the voice in your head.

Step #3—Make Choices

Step #4—Take Responsibility

Step #5—Stop Trying and Start BE-ing

Now please know that all of these steps are not going to happen over night. Each and every one of them requires time, practice, and patience. Michael Jordon didn't master his world renowned dunk in a day! He knew that it would require time, practice and patience. So, now that we are at the end this chapter, do you understand what I mean when I say, not being bothered by your haters is merely a bonus. If you use all of these steps or just focus on one, I guarantee you that your life, is getting ready to be off the hook like never before. From here on out, you got it. This is YOUR life, because *You* are being *You*.

Now that you have that under your belt my next question to you is….

3

Who's got your back?

One of the things that come with the territory of high school and college is the group of friends you hang out with. Whether the friends are from your previous school, extra-curricular activities or even in your neighborhood, there tends to be a group of people that you will hang with. This is something I think is very important in school and your life overall.

Think about it. Is it really healthy to go through 3 or 4 years of your life not getting know anyone? Sounds like a lonely journey doesn't it? Then let me pose this question. When it comes to the friends you surround yourself with, is it about quantity? Is it more important to have 2 friends or 25 friends? Do you like a lot of people around you? Do you like to hang in a group or just hang with that one good friend?

Okay, so then the ultimate question is how do *you* define friend? Are there certain qualities you are looking for in a person? While I was in school I met my buddy Philly. I had gotten fed up with so called friends or what I like to call "part time" friends. It seemed like the only time these people wanted to hang out with me or chat was when they wanted to be bothered. However, whenever I needed someone to talk to and just sit back and blow off some steam, they were either too busy or just weren't around. One day I got so fed up with the part-timers that I decided to sit down and make a wish list of the qualities I wanted my future friends to have.

The qualities:

- Someone who is supportive

- Fun to hang around

- Serious when needed

- Own sense of self, and

- Could be real with me without trying to tear me down.

These were the standards I set. To some of you, it may seem like a lot to ask for and for some of you it may not be enough. But this list was for me, myself, and I. These were the expectations set for my new found friends to be. I had no clue where they would come from, where I would meet them, or how soon it would be. I just made up in my mind to search for these qualities in my friends.

Throughout your education from high school to college, as a matter of fact, throughout your entire life, you are going to constantly meet different people. Some will be familiar and friendly. Some will be distant and cold. No matter if they are nice or not, the fact is, unless you lock yourself away in a closet, have someone bolt the door shut, build a brick wall in front of it, then put a sign on it that says "Do not open!" you are going to meet new people. The good thing about this is some of these people will become your friends.

There are two secrets to share with you that can make or break your career in school. Secret # 1—Know your friends. Secret # 2—Build a team of friends. Or as I like to say, build the crew that's got your back? Now, what I mean by this is not who's got your back when you are getting into a fight or someone who's got your back when you are getting ready to ask that dream person out for that dream date. This group is there to help you make your time in school great, easy and FUN! There are all kinds of people out there who could do it. Then there are friends who are always there, nothing special, nothing exciting, but they are just there and they got your back no matter what.

This group of people is who I like to call my "Crew." Or even if I am feeling really off the chain, I call them my "Posse." Some may call it a team, their boys, their girls, homies, homeboys, homegirls, their dawgs or something to that affect. But all in all it is a group of people who you hang with right? Cool.

Here's some news for you. Whether you are in school, a special club, or in life period, the crew you have can make or break your progress. So how do we determine that? Easy! But before we determine how your crew can make or break you, let's find out who they are. Get out a pen or pencil and some paper.

You set? Or are you reading past this point saying "I'll do it later." Caught cha! NOW GET THE PAPER! Also, you want to have a watch or clock nearby.

On the next page, for a minute straight, non stop, write out all the names of the people you consider your friends, associates or a part of your crew. You ready? On your mark ... Get Set ... GO! (Enter Jeopardy Music Here) OK, times up! Was this easy or hard for you?

Take a look at the list of people you wrote down. Out of this list of people, circle the top 3 to 5 friends that you know you want to be a part of your crew for sure. Now if you only have 1 or 2 that's fine.

The next step for each of them is to list 5 of their best qualities. After you write out the 5 qualities about them, what seems to be the theme in all of your friends? Do they all share the same qualities or are they all totally different? What do you see in your friends who make up the crew? Are they funny? Adventurous? Focused? Talented? What is it?

Before we move on, I have a bonus for you. I invite you to do this list of 5 qualities for all the people on your list, or at least another 5. Trust me, if you do this exercise full out, you are going to unveil some remarkable stuff. Some may be what you expected and others may be very surprising.

Ok, now that you have had a chance to ask yourself some serious questions about people who are in your crew, you have probably noticed that there are some people who should not be there. It's almost like playing that game "What does not belong." Some of us learned that game when we were kids, but didn't carry it over into our real life.

Looking at your crew, have you found someone that does not belong? Are some not very supportive of your or your dream? Are some only around you when you partake in some habits that are not beneficial to you like drinking alcohol, doing drugs, or even having sex? Are some only there because they feel you are their ticket to becoming popular? Are they constantly putting you down and saying what you can't do? Do you find that they lie to you? Okay, here's one for you, are they a hatah? If you answered yes to any of these, that person is what I call **Toxic**.

No matter how you cut, there will always be people in your life that includes, good, bad and toxic. So just like toxic waste is bad for everyone so are toxic people. Toxic people can be the most unsupportive, unforgiving, dream snatching, putting down, non caring people you will ever meet.

My share of toxic people has driven me to be very cautious of whom I let be a part of my crew. Don't get me wrong, everyone is allowed a chance. But what if they take that chance and screw it up so bad? What do you do? The answer? Only you can decide what that is. But let me share a story with you.

I met a buddy in high school. We were so cool. We hung out all the time, always looked good, always knew the right people, were the best in our extra curricular activities, we were like blood brothers. We both graduated from high school and went out pursuing our different ventures in life. I was on my way to college and he was on a mission to land a good job for a year then go to college. We lived about 45 minutes away from each other and because neither one of us had a car, and our Mom's wouldn't let us drive theirs, we would communicate over the phone and computer a lot.

We grew apart a little bit, but not much. As we got older and we got our own cars moved into our own places, we became really close and started hanging out more. But somewhere along the line, things started to change. He was not around as much. It was hard to get in touch with him and we went days, weeks and in some cases months without talking. But being a forgiving person every time we got back in touch, he apologized and we got along like nothing even happened. But even with that, it seemed like his stories would change from one day to the next. One day it would be "well, yeah, I went to that party and it was nice." Then a few weeks later the same party would come up in a conversation and he would say "I don't remember telling you I went to that party." The more time went on, the more I started realizing that he was not being honest with me 100%. Of course when I started seeing this, I started to distance myself a little bit unsure of how to handle it.

A few years later I started dating one of his good friends and we hit it off very well. Can you say really *really* cute? So I don't know if he was a bit jealous or what, but my friend started acting funny. Not directly towards me, but he just wasn't that same blood brother I knew some years back. Well, the longer I was in the relationship with his friend, the more I would hear conflicting stories. He would tell me one thing, then, tell my partner another thing. This whole dishonesty thing was starting to wear me out and wear me thin (and I'm a pretty big guy). But trying to give him the benefit of the doubt, I felt like I should remain his best friend, no matter what.

About a year later, I got a phone call from him out of the blue. I mean, by this time, we talked maybe twice a month. So he called and said he needed to tell me something really important. So I was available to talk. After a few minutes of conversation, he lowered the boom "A'ric, I found out that I am HIV positive." My heart stopped. I felt like there was no air in the room and tears started to well up in my eyes. "What? When did you find this out?" I asked.

He shared with me the whole story. He went on to tell me how it hurt and how he was a bit depressed about it, but he would make it through. I offered him 100% support. Whatever he needed me to do to help him get through this I would be there for him. He accepted the offer and we chatted for a little longer before we got off the phone. When we did, I knew in my heart that I was willing to give him the support he needed. A few days later, I gave him a call to check on him. He didn't answer so I left a message. A few days later, I made another call. Again, no answer, so I left another message. After calling several times, I started to get really concerned. I didn't know if he couldn't handle the pressures of what he knew and just decided he wanted to end his life or jump off the bridge. I had no clue of what was going on and it was freaking me out! The only thing I knew was that he was dealing with this and he was alone.

4 months later I got a call out of the blue from him. Of course I wanted to know if he was ok, but then after that I lost it. I may have lost it a bit much, but I was screaming into the phone with tears running down my eyes "don't you ever scare me like that again! I didn't know what happened to you." His response was simply "Sorry. I'll do better next time." We kept in contact for a few weeks then he disappeared again. I got to the point where I didn't want to have him as a friend anymore. This may sound really harsh and selfish, but this was only because I was looking out for him, but he wasn't looking out for me.

Several months later, out of the blue he showed up to my job … yep, he surely did and gave me the same "I'm sorry, I'll get better" speech which grew old with me. But with him this time came a business proposition. Long story short, I liked the proposition, followed through with it, then all of a sudden, he was no longer around to help me with it. Without warning he was just gone, and left me hanging with this all by myself. And along with that was a side order of dishonesty as well. This was a friendship that I had deemed no longer and wrote him off as being toxic. We talk every once in a while here and there, but the friendship is long gone. If you were in my shoes, what would you have done? Do you have any friends like this who show these symptoms or any clues that they may be toxic?

If so, do you think it is good for them to be a part of your crew? Sometimes, throughout high school, you are going to be forced to look at matters from a long-term perspective. By long term I do not mean 20 to 30 years but long term being anything over 5 to 10 years. Can you look at those next few years and see how that toxic person could bring you down?

So what do you do when you discover the toxic people? Again, that is your call. (I can see some body reading this saying "I wish he would stop saying that.") As much as I would like to say just kick them out of your life, it is not always that simple. But in all fairness to you, you have to let them go. It is your choice. Do you want to put up with the shenanigans? Or do you want to make your life better and know how to let them go? If so, keep reading. If not, still keep reading you may need this for future reference.

LETTING GO OF THE TOXIC PEOPLE

There are two ways of letting go of toxic people. They are what I like to call "releases." You have a *Hard Release* and a *Soft Release*.

Let's look at a "Soft Release" first. This is what you would do when you want to keep a friend or someone on your crew. You don't want them to be out of your life, but you have to bring some things to the forefront. Let's say you have a friend who is cool to be around, but whenever you start talking about your future, they become so negative. You have come to wits end with it and you have reached a point where you question if this person is really "toxic."

After reviewing the friendship that you two have you decide that this person overall is a good person to be around, but the negative vibe has to got to stop. This is where the Soft Release comes into play. What you would do is pull that friend to the side in confidence and just let them know straight up that you think they are cool to be around, but what is not cool is the negative vibe. From that point you can decide how you want to explain what is wrong and how it is affecting you.

Two things you should be very careful of with this conversation. First, you must be honest! Sometimes people think that in order to be honest, you have to be rude. That is not true. If you approach your friend in a manner that is not tactful, don't expect them to be tactful with you. Second, you may catch some detest from your friend. They may feel like you are attacking them. During this time you have to reassure them, that you want their friendship, but you want the negative part of it to cease. But both of these points are very critical. If you are not 100% honest and you are trying to sugar coat how you really feel, you are setting yourself up for a less desirable friendship than what you had before, simply because you are now walking around knowing that you had the chance to say what you felt, but you didn't take it.

After having this conversation, tell them that you respect what you two have as friends and instead of just giving up the friendship overall, you want to work at it. Usually, this let's them know that you are not trying to be rude or mean, just real.

Caution—When someone feels attacked, what do they do usually? Attack back? You guessed it. If this person is snapping back at you for being real and speaking how you feel, maybe this conversation was needed to reveal if you should move it from a soft release to a "Hard Release." How can you be true friends with someone if you can't come to them and speak your mind honestly? Don't you deserve to have a friend where you can be you?

You'll here me refer to my friend Phillie. I promise you, if I didn't know my mother and his mother, I would have thought we were separated at birth. We are so close that when we tell people we are brothers, they flip out when they find we are not biological brothers, we just adopted each other. He and I have had some of the best times and craziest moments. He and I have also had some very serious moments. But I do recall one time that some where out of the blue, he was not feeling our friendship. I really couldn't understand why because I thought I hadn't done anything. Come to find out, there was a disagreement between him and someone I was dating at the time. The way it went down, I thought everything was cool, but he ended up with some hurt feelings, which he didn't share with me right away.

Now if you knew anything about my friend Phillie, you would know that if he is not feeling your vibe, you both can be standing in the room, and he will make you feel like you are invisible and he doesn't see you. Finally getting down to the bottom of this, I had to take the *Soft Release* approach with him. I came to him and asked him "What's Up? What's wrong? Are you mad at me about something?" From there we had a discussion that revealed some misunderstandings. Now I could have gone to him snapping off and not listening, and lost him as a friend forever. But because I knew he was a friend that I wanted to be a part of my crew and my life for a long time, I took the Soft Release approach. Because I took that approach, we are back to acting crazy. As a matter of fact crazier than before. That is my boy! Love you man!

Now let's talk about a *Hard Release*. The Hard Release is when you have absolutely made up your mind you no longer want to deal with this so called friend. They have been negative, not supportive, they are liar, or they are just a plain ole' hatah. You approach this person and just let them know, that you think it is probably best that you two no longer be friends or hang out together. I am going to full warn you, they are going to feel attacked. They may feel like they are not good enough to be your friend. Let them know that the two of you are just on different pages. There may be some debate, there may not be.

Somewhere along the line, they are going to ask you why. When they give you this opportunity, don't back down. If your why is because you feel that they always have something negative to say, or they are just always dragging you down, let them know. There will be some people who have no clue that they are like this. They might even be surprised to hear this. Again, like in the soft release, you have to be careful how you approach this, but being careful does not mean you give up being real.

Fair warning, in attack mode, the toxic person is going to lash out at you! You are probably going to be called names, and will probably be talked about. Are you okay with that? I mean, you don't have to be okay with it but are you ready for that? Around this area a lot of people say, "you know what I should do a 'soft release' to keep it peaceful." Guess what, been there, done that, and bought the t-shirt. I know we want to be cautious of other people's feelings, but what about yours? No, life is not ALL about you, but it is a great deal about you and the people you have around you.

Do you want to continue a friendship with someone who is always dragging you down? Maybe they are not dragging you down directly, but whenever they come around they always have something negative or nasty to say. I mean how crazy is that? You waste more time and energy trying to fight the negative energy than actually enjoying the friendship.

A Hard Release is not the easiest thing to do, but sometimes for the sake of you, your life and your future, you have to take the hard way and just do it. Have I taken the hard release with people? Yes! Most definitely. I mentioned my friend earlier who would be here today and gone tomorrow. He resurfaced eventually. When he did, I took the Hard Release approach with. I was very up front and very direct. Did he get it? Yes. Do we still talk on occasion? Yes. Then there have even been times when I have been at a really high point in my life and instead my friend being happy for me, they revealed every negative aspect about it. I was so crushed that I almost didn't want to keep on. But then I had to stop and realize that it was either me, or that person. Guess who I chose? Without doubt! Me!

So, now you know what a Soft and Hard Release is. In most cases, you may take the Soft Release approach. Then in some, you are going to have to really look at the Hard Release approach. Then there will be times where you would just need to take a chill pill and speak with your friend in the morning. Don't worry. It's all good all because it is your choice. Now let's move on. I got some things I want to tell you about.

Outside of High School, life can be fun, crazy, and tough all at the same time. Then we you add being in school to the equation, WHEWWEEE!!! Watch Out Now!!!! It can be an experience that will either drive you to be better or drive you into the ground.

By now, most of you know who your crew is or who you want your crew to be. That's cool. I applaud you on that. Can you imagine going through school alone and no friends? Let me offer a suggestion that might add some spice and flava to your crew. Your crew will consist of friends and probably family which is cool. I know outside of friends, a lot of my crew is made up of family members like my Mom, Dad, Sister and Cousins. It's off the chain and I love my crew. The for sure have my back.

Question for you? You want to make your school experience easier? Good, so let's talk about something that you can add to your Bag-O-Tricks. Have you ever considered having a mentor? Yes a mentor. Having a mentor doesn't mean that has to be someone who is 30 years older than you. As a matter of fact the mentors I speak about are even some people you may take class with or see in the halls at school.

Some of you may see this word and think "YEAH! I got one of dem!" Some of you maybe thinking "that's too much work." And some of you maybe thinking "I am the bomb-diggity, why would I need a mentor?" In my life I have found that mentors can be this great and wonderful experience or it can be a nightmare on your street. There are two types of mentors. Good & Bad! It's just that simple.

GOOD MENTORS VS. BAD MENTORS

Good mentors are people who are in your field of interest and/or has something to offer you that will help you in the future. What makes this mentor good? They can be considered an expert in what they do or just be exceptional at all they do.

A good mentor is one who is willing to impart and share with *no strings attached*. From knowledge, to experiences, to offering advice, the mentor is about giving you information and sharing stories that will assist you in being what you want to become.

A good mentor will challenge you. Why would you even waste your time to seek out a mentor if you were not ready to be challenged to get better? That's almost like going to Michael Jordan and saying, "hey Mike, I wanna get better at my game, but don't challenge me because I might not want to play anymore. Cool? Cool." Can you imagine that? A good mentor is going to give you things to do or think about that are going to push you out of your comfort zone. If you want to be the best and have the best, whatever it is, it is going to come with a challenge. So why not get some of that challenge advice from someone who's got your back or is in your crew?

What is a Bad mentor? Someone who does not have a great connection to what it is you are seeking mentorship about. Example? You are asking someone who makes $25,000.00 a year how to become a millionaire? I have been known to have a smart mouth sometimes and I know that situations like this I MUST stay away from. Because if it were me getting advice from someone like that my first question would be "well, why aren't you a millionaire yet if you have all this knowledge?" Their response would probably begin "Well, what had happened was…."

Another sign of a bad mentor? They will partially share some things with you. They don't believe in giving out the tricks of the trade or sharing with you 100%. They want to leave you guessing. They don't want you to know it all. These type of mentors, watch out for. They will make you feel as if you are getting everything you need to know, then all of a sudden, you realize that you could be learning every thing on your own.

Now let me mention that there may be cases where you will be asked to do certain things in exchange for the mentorship. But more often than not, it will be tied directly into what you will be learning. It is very much like Mr. Miyagi and the Karate Kid. I mean this man had him painting houses, fences, washing and waxing cars … I know if it were me, I would have looked at him like "Old Man You Crazy! I don't even paint! I pay someone to do it for me. I am headed to the burger joint." And then I would have thrown up my two fingers representing the Peace symbol and exited stage left.

Of course, the Karate Kid got to that point where he was ready to snap off! As soon as he did Mr. Miyagi made him realize that all the work he was doing was teaching him some foundational principles to fight.

With that in mind there may come a time where your mentor will ask you do to certain things. Trust your judgment. If you feel this is going too far, then address it. It is okay to ask your mentor "why are we doing this?" If they give you a vague answer or try to degrade you because you asked, then you might need to reconsider mentors.

Another sign of a bad mentor is when they make you feel as if you owe them something. Be *very* careful of these folks because they are out there. If you approach someone about becoming your mentor and they accept the offer under the conditions that you have to do something out of the ordinary for them, **BACK OFF!!!!!** Generally, when someone is asked to be a mentor, it is taken as an honorable notion. You would be amazed at how many people would jump at the opportunity of mentoring all because they want to impart their knowledge. But if you approach a mentor and they are telling you things like "I will tell you this information, if you go out on a date with me." Or "I will give you information if you cut my lawn for the next two summers" really look at that. Is that a route you want to go?

So now, let's talk about how to select mentors to add to your crew. There are a few questions you need to ask yourself before you set out to choose a mentor.

- Why do you want a mentor?

- What do you want to accomplish by having a mentor?

- What do you want to learn from that mentor?

- Are you ready to take the instructions and even criticism from mentors?

HOW DO YOU BEGIN TO CHOOSE A MENTOR?

There is a method to the madness of choosing a mentor. At first it can seem like a tough task but after getting into it you can easily make fun out of it and then make your crew off the chain with some of the greatest support your world has ever seen.

So here are the steps:

Step # 1—Decide on your *why*:

What brings you to want a mentor? Is it so you can improve in a certain area? Are you looking to shorten your learning curve by selecting a mentor who can give you advice around the work to be done? Keep scoping questions like this and when you find a *why* that gets you excited, stick with that one and remind yourself throughout the entire process this is why the mentor is in your crew.

Step # 2—Find role models:

Start off by looking at people who you consider role models in the area in which are seeking a mentor. An example would be, if you are on a freshman team for athletics, are there any varsity players who you would like to emulate? Who catches your eye? Who do you want to be like? "Like Mike?"

Step # 3—Do your research:

Take time to do your own research. If it is drama that you are looking for a role-model in, you may want to study some of the plays that you have seen your role model in. Get the script and read over it. Find a scene that caught your attention that your role model performed. Then research that person as much as you can without seeming like a stalker. What time do they get to school? When do they rehearse? How often do they rehearse? When you get information like this ahead of time, it makes for a better situation because you will know when and when not to approach someone.

Step # 4—Approach your role-model:

After doing your research you may discover some things like your role model gets to school early and has breakfast before classes begin. Or know that your role model does not like to talk on the phone but loves to check e-mail. Knowing this helps you to approach this person. For some the approach may be easy, for others it may be difficult. But approach them. Remember, this is to help you become a better you. Once you know how to approach them, **be direct**. There is nothing like someone coming up to you saying "hey looks like you're having some hot cereal this morning, smells good…. cereal that's hot … smells good." Before you know it you are standing there sounding like Forrest Gump, but the only difference is, Forrest Gump is making way more sense than what you are sounding like now. When you approach them, introduce yourself if they don't already know you. After that introduction, go right into letting them know that you are interested in them being one of your mentors. When you have gotten it all out there on the table, let them talk. Wait for their response to what you have just asked them. Heads up! Some are going to ask you "why." When you know your why, you are able to be direct and to the point. Also, knowing your why ahead of time and communicating that will impress the mentor. They will you have put some effort into this whole process.

Step # 5—Stick to your agreement:

Okay, so the mentor agreed to take you on and you two have worked out the details of this relationship. Maybe it means you two will meet once a month and sit and talk about some ideas to become better.

Maybe you will meet every week to get together for some training, or maybe they may ask you to do some research. What ever it is, stick to your agreement. This is the one place where you can lose a mentor as quick as you gain one. Remember they are where you want to be. They don't have to work at having what they have because they are already there. They are going to help you. Just be careful, because if you don't stick to your agreements, it may be viewed as you not taking the work seriously. And when they feel you are not taking it seriously, it could mean a waste of time to them. Do not fall into this trap.

There you have it, the 5 steps of finding and securing your mentor to be on your crew. This leads me to the next thing that is notorious in school. It is found mostly in high school, but it can be found almost any where. Drum roll please!!! Peer Pressure! Ok, those two words are so cliché nowadays, but it is a group of words that hold a lot of power behind them, and if you don't look out for it or know what it looks like when it comes, it can get you in a sticky situation.

WHAT IS PEER PRESSURE?

I thought it was a good idea to introduce peer pressure in this chapter because a lot of times the peer pressure doesn't come from people who we don't like. Think about it. If some mean girl you didn't like, came up to you and said "hey you, rob that store for me and get me some cigarettes while you're in there" you would look at her like she flew over the cuckoo's nest. However, when it comes to our friends or associates, and even our crew, we tend to take it to heart.

So what is Peer Pressure? Peer pressure is when some people in your life are able to steer you in a particular direction of doing or saying something. If you do not cooperate with the request, usually, there is some type of "pressure" put on you to do what the peers want you to do. So with that being said, is all Peer Pressure bad?

A DIFFERENT TAKE ON PEER PRESSURE

We have all heard about peer pressure in a negative light. Peer pressure is usually used to introduce scenarios like your friends wanting you to smoke a cigarette or some marijuana "because it is cool." The peers may want you to drink at a party that you all went to "to impress the people there." Or they may want you to try a new drug "because you are friends and you are suppose to try new things together." These are just a few of the scenarios of negative peer pressure.

Now what a lot of people don't talk about is positive peer pressure. The definition of peer pressure remains the same, but the difference is you are being led in a direction to do good or be better. During my Junior and Senior year in High School, I was a member of the video team. We did the morning announcements via television and would also give little tid-bits about what was going on in the community.

The show ran daily and each show required a main anchor, a person who covered events, and a person who covered sports. We were the high school version of your typical morning news show. There were 5 anchors. Each anchor had their own day and pretty much had control over the production of the show. I was the anchor for Friday's show. Thinking about it makes me laugh because the name of my show was A.N.T. Productions. A.N.T. stood for A'ric, Natalie and Tony. Natalie covered events (*who was the girl that every one thought was geeky at first, but they got to know her and love her*), and Tony covered Sports (*he was the popular quarterback at the school who had a charming personality and the camera loved him*).

We made an awesome group together. Now because all of the anchors knew each other and we were cool with each other, we always had this competition going on. It had to have been one of the quietest competitions ever, because we never said outright "we are competing." But one thing that was interesting with us, we always challenged each other to produce a better show each week.

I had it pretty easy because I got to see everyone's show through-out the week, and then bring the noise or snap off on that Friday! Being in the studio was so much fun when these silent competitions went on, because to the entire school, we all got along on and off the camera. However, in the studio after each show it would go a little something like this. "And cut ... That's a wrap, great show Thursday crew." Says the producer. The Thursday anchor jumps up and says "YEAH BOYEE!!!! What you got on that Friday Huh? Top That!" And then the Thursday crew would all do their happy dance and laugh to celebrate their show. "That's cool, that's cool! Wait till tomorrow" Tony from the Friday show said calmly. "Ain't nothing but a G Thang! Nothing but 2 chicken wings in a bucket with bar-b-que sauce on it. We got this!" I would state as I walked into the pro-ducers booth to avoid having something thrown at me because I knew I was talking trash.

This became a tradition for us. That type of pressure though fun, *was* peer pressure. All of the anchors and hosts had developed a bond with each other over the school year. Yet, it was this type of pressure that would make everyone step up to the plate and just do their "thang" for their show. Even with all the trash talking, throwing of paper and people trying to jump on each other's back, this was posi-tive peer pressure to do better and be better for each new week. The final result the whole school witnessed greatly produced shows that rocked more and more as the weeks went on.

With this positive peer pressure, we helped each other so much during the journey of high school career. I can even recall times out-side of the studio where if one of the crew was having a hard time either with school or problems at home, we came together to help each other out. It was like this quiet fraternity/sorority of News anchors. There was a time when I had a death in the family that was a bit hard for me to handle. I remember crying and one of the other anchors was there and held my hand for at least an hour. That was one of the best things. I truly felt like a group of people had my back and genuinely cared about me.

So, recap here, stay away from the negative peer pressure. You know what it is! Do not act dumb when it shows up. Really, if you are hanging out with some of your friends, buddies, crew, posse, homies whatever you want to call them, and they ask you to do something that falls into the bonehead category ... Uhh, you might want to rethink that.

Just in case you are unsure of what they are, the bonehead categories include shoplifting, trying drugs, drinking alcohol, having sex, talking about other people, getting into a fight, egging somebody's car, decorating someone's house with toilet paper or something that is just *soooooo* stupid like chugging a bottle of spicy horseradish sauce. And if it is something that you have to question MIGHT be in the bonehead category ... it probably is.

So that's negative peer pressure. Right? Okay, got it? Now keep in mind, if you have some friends who are constantly offering negative peer pressure, it's time to check yourself. Are you willing to risk crazy consequences for something stupid? I mean really who wants to sit in jail for egging someone's car? Sorry, I have no desire and I hope you have no desire to be locked in a jail cell next a man named "Big Tiny" who stands 6'11 300 pounds and has a high pitched squeaky voice. Or sitting next to Nancie "Know No Good" Drew who sounds like what "Big Tiny" should sound like and has a twitching eye. Not for 1 day, not even for 10 minutes. No thank you.

Now when it comes to positive peer pressure, it's all good. Just look at is as healthy competition. My experiences with it constantly drove me to become a better person. Life is about growth and change right? I mean really, imagine yourself being the exact same person, doing the exact same thing, and looking the exact same way 10 years from now. Inspiring? I don't think so.

Have a crew i.e. your peers in life that present challenges to you to make you a better person and in turn you can help someone to become a better person. It is a wonderful cycle! As matter of fact, it is awesome.

So when it comes to peer pressure, don't look at it one way. There are two types, but only you can define if the scenario is negative or positive. It's your call. And just like your minutes on your cell phone, use them well or suffer the consequences of the bill.

So, we've looked at who your crew is, the people we can add to the crew, even how to release people from your crew. We've covered a lot. Creating the right crew may not be easy but is so worth the work. You have to go out there and in some cases meet people you've never met before. Sometimes, it will be uncomfortable to ask people to step off your crew, but guess what? In the long run it is all better for you. Big city to small town, it doesn't matter. You could have gone to school with the same people for the last ten years, but that does not mean they have to be your friends just for that reason.

From some of the examples given to you earlier, you can clearly see that you are given a choice. In life just to know that you can choose who your friends are is *huge*! But my question to you is how will you choose? Will you choose people for friendship because of the way they dress? Will you choose them because they are the most popular? Or will you choose those who can be a good friend to you, be there for you in hard times, not try to do anything STUPID that would get everyone in trouble, and even challenge you to step up your game whether it is in school, an activity or even life period. The choice is yours. So what do you choose?

THE SECRET IS ...

Before I close out this chapter, there is a secret I would like to share with you regarding your crew. Let's say you have the dream team crew. They are so good, that when you look at them, all you can do is say "Shucky Ducky Quack Quack! My Crew Is ALL THAT!!!" *(Don't laugh at me, I just get goofy like that sometimes)*. When you have a crew that is this great, you want to keep them right? So what is the secret to keeping them?

Don't Wait To Appreciate!

It can be one of the best feelings in the world to know that you have a group of people who has your back one way or another. To know that you have friends who support you in something as serious as pursuing your dream, or even as simple as getting a really good laugh in, having this crew can be a great time in life.

So, once you have you have them ... don't take them for granted. Most of your crew is there because they want to be. Not because you are forcing them to be. This group of people helps you, supports you, makes you laugh because they want to, not because they are required to. You don't cut them a check do you? (*If you do cut them a check, I think you should reread chapter 1 about 3 times before you continue.*) With that being said, take time to appreciate your crew. Sometimes it is just a great gesture to stop and say "you know what, you are really crazy, but I really appreciate your friendship and the support that you give." When was the last time, you have said something like this to someone who offers you their friendship, support and love? You would be amazed at how showing your appreciation can build a greater friendship. Not only because you stopped to say "I don't care what anyone else says, you are cool ..." Sometimes it is just good to be good to some one who is good to you.

It is too easy to take your crew for granted. We take their support, encouragement, even tough love, but when do we say or show our appreciation for it? There is never a "perfect" time to share this with someone in your life. However, it is important to share it. Whenever you do, share it without expecting anything back. You don't have to wait until the right time. As a matter of fact don't wait. You would be amazed at the reaction of some of your friends. Just keep this in mind.

A part of my crew was one of my Aunts. She was one of the funniest, most rowdiest women I **loved** to be around. She had a very youthful and fun spirit. Growing up I used to think she was mean because to me, it seemed like she never smiled. Some days I would look at her and say to myself "why does she look so mean?" However, as I got older, I got to know her. Growing up, my mom would always get my hair cut really *really* short to avoid having to go to the barbershop all the time. I would look at myself in the mirror and call myself Mr. Clean.

One day after I got my hair cut, I happened to go over to my Aunt's house. "Whew! Look at that head!" she yelled. No "hello," no "how are you doing," just as soon as I walked through the door she launched into the big-headed boy story which I happen to be the main character of.

"Com'ere" (translation come here) she said.

"What?" I said sheepishly.

"Com'ere" she demanded.

I made my way over to her in her. The next thing you know all I heard and felt was a big WHACK! That was the sound my head and her hand made when my she slapped me across the back of my head.

"Nothing like slapping a clean headed boy!" she chuckled.

Only because she was my aunt, and I knew she was known to be a fighter, and her son was like 4 feet taller than me, did I not hit her in the back of her head. After the sting wore off, I settled down. Needless to say, that became a tradition between her and I.

Some years later, she shared with the family that the doctors discovered that she had breast cancer. Though it was a rough blow to her and the family, she still managed to keep it upbeat and keep our tradition alive.

One day, I was in the area where she lived and I decided "you know what, I'm going to go buy her some flowers, just because." So off to local grocery store I went to pick up some flowers. I called her on my cell phone.

"Hello" she said sounding like I woke her up.

"Are you decent?" I asked.

"Am I decent? Who is this?"

"That's a shame you don't even know your nephews voice." I sighed.

"Oh boy, it's you. What you want?"

"Can I stop by, I got something for you."

"You got some food?" she inquired.

"No it's not food." I laughed.

"Oh well, Okay, I guess you can come over."

It wasn't even a few minutes later when I pulled into her driveway. I hopped out the car and ran to her door and rang the door bell like I was a mad man. "Boy what is your problem" she screamed on the other side of the door. All I could do was laugh.

She opened the door and I followed her in. We shared our tradition. Luckily over the years, she didn't do it so hard, or I just got accustomed to it.

"Ta-Dum!" I said as I whipped the flowers from behind my back. They were Casablanca's Pretty white lilies. Her face brightened up and she asked "what are these for?"

"No Reason, just because I love you."

She got quiet for a moment. For one to know my aunt, these moments did not come often. After a brief pause she kept saying, "thank you, thank you, thank you." It felt good to brighten up her day with a surprise just to show her I loved and appreciated her. She was a true member of my crew. She always pushed me to be better, do greater, live harder and that was just who she was to me.

About a week later, I got a call that my aunt had been hospitalized. Apparently, the cancer took a turn for the worse. She was placed in a hospital downtown Chicago, which was not too far from where I worked at the time. I talked to my Mom and told her I would stop by the hospital and drop off some flowers. My mom immediately let me know that no flowers or balloons were accepted on that floor.

My initial reaction was upset and hurt. Why couldn't I bring my aunt some flowers? After I calmed down a bit, my mind went back to the surprise visit. In that moment I was comforted realizing that it didn't take her to go into the hospital for me to show her appreciation by buying her flowers. This moment of my life will always be remembered, simply because it was the last conversation I had with my aunt before she passed.

Sharing this story is a bit rough for me because it makes me realize how much I miss my Aunt and what I would give to have her share that tradition of slapping me on my head one last time.

With that being said, don't ever wait to show your crew your appreciation & love for being there for you in your life. It's not that hard. Gestures of flowers or a gift are great, but sometimes all it takes is simply saying to your crew "I appreciate you and I thank you for being here." You would be amazed at how people will respond to this.

You could have one of the best crews in the world. But if you don't show your appreciation to them, though they may be the best, it may be one of the most short-lived crews. When was the last time you took time to appreciate?

So with that being said, I want to know who's really got your back? This experience only comes once in a lifetime. But it is through this experience that you can find a life time friend. Don't take who you surround yourself with lightly. As I said earlier, your crew can either make you or break you. Myself, I want to be made with the greatest crew ever! So now that you know what it takes, Don't Be Scurred ... move on to Chapter 4.

4

Don't Be Scurred!

So really, what is holding you back from being the next best person that this world could ever see? Have any idea? Does it have anything to do with what you look like? What school you go to? How about the friends that you have? Family? Or better yet, you? Are you your main enemy? Some of you may be saying to yourself "no, not me."

Well, I'll put it to you this way, if you have done every single thing that you have ever wanted to do in your life, stop reading here, put the book up and give Oprah a call. She may be looking for a guest of your caliber on her next show. Really, I mean it.

Now for those of you, including myself, who have always wanted to do something, but for some reason, you didn't do it, keep reading, I have a good clue on why. There was a point in my life where I was so convinced that I did not do or have all the things that I wanted because of other people. Yep, other people were the blame for me not having what I wanted in my life. However, after some time passed, I realized that life was what you made it, and I got really clear about who was responsible for my life, (i.e. me); Through reality checks and just general observation, I quickly unveiled the thing that was holding me back. I mentioned earlier that we can be our own worst enemy. But why? Why do we become our own enemies? It's not like one morning we woke up, jumped out of bed and ran the mirror and said "you looking for an enemy? WELL YOU FOUND IT! AND I AM GOING TO BE THE WORST YOU HAVE EVER SEEN!" Now if you have done this, stop reading this and give Oprah a call, I am quite sure she is looking for guest of your caliber.

When it all boils down to it, the source of it all is a four letter word that spells F-E-A-R, FEAR. This is the driving force of us being our own enemy. Can you think of some things in your life that have happened, or you have seen, that made you act out of fear?

Fear is not a fun thing to deal with. Fear can take a toll on anyone including some of the most successful people in this world. It doesn't matter how old you are, your gender status, class, race, body size or shape, fear searches for a home where it can reside and rule and that home is usually found in your thoughts.

There are two ways that fear can affect you. First is mentally. Think about it. Where is fear? What does it look like? Is it wearing some jeans, white gym shoes, and a T-Shirt saying "I'm Here! I'm Fear! Get over it!" When it comes to some of us, you would think that fear is standing right behind us at 6'9 428 pounds *(of solid muscle I might add)* who demands your every move. This is the problem. A lot of us treat fear like it is this character that will pulverize us if we do not do whatever it says. We make it this being in our world that can physically cause harm.

Yet, when we look at it closely, fear is just merely in our minds. In fact, fear cannot be seen. However, what is seen are the *results* of fear. But, we never *see* fear. So what is fear? Fear is just a thought. That's all it really is. When fear becomes a driving force in your life it is because you are letting fear into your thoughts constantly. Earlier we talked about the voice in your head and you being two different entities. A lot of people walk around thinking they are that voice in their head. So here is a way to look at fear. Fear is merely a DJ that is hosting a show on your 24/7 personal radio station. That's it! So, where does fear get its power? From us! It gets its power when we allow it to morph from a thought to some kind of reality. The key here is *us*. We allow the fear to be. From thought, we materialize it with action, thus producing a result which in turn makes it reality.

Now, let me be clear about fear. There are times when our actions or reactions toward fear are extremely valid. Would fear raise up in you if you were in a burning house? Of course it would. Would fear take over if you saw a grizzly bear approaching? Heck yeah! Would fear visit you when you introduce your boyfriend or girlfriend to your parents? YEAH!!! Fear is a very natural part of a human being. The instances above are not an issue. As a matter of fact, fear is always going be with you. Just like your wonderful voice inside your head that plays on your personal radio station 24/7. Be very aware of that. I have been speaking across the country for almost 10 years and do you know fear still rises up in me right before I go on stage. Depending on when you catch me, Fear will raise up in me so tough that I get scared, nervous and sometimes downright nauseous. There are times where you may catch me bent over trying to catch my breath right before I go on stage. So again, it is a very valid thing to experience, even when you are experienced at doing something. Feel me?

When does fear strike you the most? In public while speaking? During the time you want to ask for a prom date? When you want to speak your mind? When you want to dance? Right before a test? Did you say yes to any of these? Did you come up with some of your own? Either way, that's great because I want to point something out. All of these instances, even including when I speak, have happened right before you are getting ready to take action on something. Whether it is public speaking, asking someone out on a date, or even asking for a higher grade, you are taking action. While you are taking this action fear is broadcasting loud and clear on your personal radio station.

When it comes to fear there is a guarantee that I am going to give you. FEAR will ALWAYS be around. Yep, no matter what you do, who you become, how much money you make, fear will always be around. Many of us do not face our fears because we believe in order for us to overcome it, we have to get rid of it. That is so not the case. If that is the case my friends, you will be waiting around for an extremely *long* time.

So now that you are a little bit ticked off with me about the lack of a magic potion to eradicate this thing we call fear, let's dig a little deeper into it. Why do we fear? Why does fear hold us back from pursuing our dreams and life's purpose? Let's start by looking at …

THE TWO MAIN CAUSES OF FEAR

Believe it or not, you can look at just about everyone's fear and discover that the underlying element is either fear of rejection or fear of the unknown.

Rejection

Okay, so if you were wondering which one of the two would be the one I live with, it is fear of rejection. Now I want to point out that I still have to check my fear at the door every once in a while. To be more precise I discovered within the past year or so, that I have a fear of success. YEAH! OF ALL THE THINGS TO BE SCARED OF, success! I know that sucks right? I will be the first to say if I had been living WITH Fear instead of IN Fear (I will explain shortly) this book you are reading would have been out earlier. I'm serious. I found every reason to not get this book done. I was too busy, had too much work do, didn't have enough sleep, not enough money, no one to plan my book release party, my hair wasn't looking right (and mind you I sport a bald head) and even stupid excuses like, my niece wanted me to play with her. She wasn't even a year old yet! I had any and every kind of reason to not complete this book.

So one day I said to myself "Self" and myself said "Yeah what's up?" I replied asking "Why am I putting this book off? I have mad support from my crew and everyone has done nothing but show me love. I know the book will be a guaranteed success. So why put it off?" After thinking about it for some time I realized I was afraid of rejection. How did I come up with that one? Well it might sound crazy, but here it goes. I didn't want anyone to read my book and not like it. I couldn't disappoint all of my supporters if I came out with a book that bit the big one. "What if they didn't like what I had to say?" "What if they didn't like the cover?" "What if they feel like I am trying to be better than them?" "What if the book is just plain old WHACK?" Sounds silly, but these are all actual thoughts that came to my mind.

All of the procrastinating and failure to follow through happened all because I thought I was going to be rejected in one way or another by all the people who loved and liked me. Playing this record over and over in my head had me pushing the deadline for the book to be out later and later ... yep and later.

Given that example, how many things in your life can you think of that connects to rejection. Did you not ask for that job because you thought you would have been rejected? What about filling out the application for the college you *really* wanted to go to, but you had this feeling that they may reject you, so you just went ahead and applied for the colleges you *knew* you would get into. See how fear of rejection can hold you back or even set you up to fail? Let's look at the other element ...

The Unknown

Why are people afraid to go into haunted houses? Do you think the answer is because of the goriness, high pitched screams, and low pitched moans? No, it's not. A large part of it is due to the fear of the unknown. It is more than the goriness. We already know it's just special effects, the actors are wearing special make-up and dressed in costumes. Yet for some reason, we freak out when we go into haunted houses.

To prove this point, I'll share an embarrassing moment with you. I vowed to keep this between my family and I, but I feel you should know. I went to a wax museum during one of my vacations. This wax museum in particular had a dungeon. In the dungeon there was a section that was called "LIVE." They called it that because it was the "haunted" portion of the Museum and had live actors in it. In other words, it was a smaller scale version of a haunted house.

For as long as I remember I have always hated haunted houses. So being bold I went in with my family. Now I thought I was going to be cool. These people were actors and the rest was make-up and costumes right? Yeah right. So I walked in being the bold one of the group and when we got in, it was so dark you could hardly see anything. All I could make out was 4 dark silhouettes in each corner of the room. Immediately fear stood right up in me and said "Alright, Fear is present, let's go!" Hearing the broadcast loud and clear I thought "okay which one is the live actor." So what did I do? I froze. I called for my father to come take the lead "Dad, you go first." So he did. While walking ahead, sure enough one of the silhouettes came alive and got right in front of us. Well, I was cool because he was in my father's face and not mine. So I'm cool, I'm strong, thinking, "I got this, if any of the actors comes up to me, I'll just be bold, stay strong and keep walking."

Well, nothing could have prepared me for what was about to happen next. Somehow, my step-mom and I got separated from my Dad and my Sister. So during this time I am really walking slow just waiting for the next actor to jump out at us. As we are walking next thing you know, a roar comes from the ceiling and so does this guy with horrible make-up! I screamed like the biggest little girl and fell back onto the ground not knowing why I was not informed that people would be hanging from the ceiling!

Why do you suppose that scared me the way that it did? It was the fear of the unknown. See once we got into the dark, I pretty much knew after awhile that the actors would be coming either from the left or the right or even behind me. I hadn't prepared for the ceiling action and at that point I felt like I was at square one all over again.

Many of us are like this when it comes to what we don't know or understand. Just like the fear of rejection, people will avoid *knowing* things instead of discovering something new or unveiling the unknown. Why does fear of the unknown get to people the way that it does? Truth? We are so accustomed to knowing everything and having everything at our fingertips, that if we don't know it or know about, it instantly becomes the "bad" thing and our Fear gauge kicks into high gear.

I personally believe this is why so many people do not travel across the country, try new foods, or even listen to different kinds of music. Fear of the unknown can keep you from experiencing life on a whole new level. When you don't experience the unknown in life, what becomes the quality of your life? We as human beings, though we don't like to admit it often, we get bored easily with the same thing over and over and over again. We are always looking and in search of the next best thing. However, if we don't satisfy the need because the fear of the unknown, you can and in some cases will literally cripple the quality of your life.

FEAR OF REJECTION & THE UNKNOWN HAND IN HAND

If you look at a lot of reality TV shows today, you are witnessing both elements of fear strongly. Let's look at some of the latest shows like America's Next Top Model (I Love You Tyra!). How does it show up here? Let's take a look. Fear of rejection: "If I pose this way, the judges may not like me" and the fear of the unknown: "will I get cut from the show today? Will I be in the bottom two? ... I don't know I can't take this pressure."

Isn't it crazy to know how much both of these fears can operate in your life and sometimes you don't even know it. It's a bit scary, but it does that. These fears will rear their ugly heads even when you don't realize them. For the next several days see which one of the two fears come up for you? Do you have fear of rejection or fear of the unknown? Word of caution, if you are starting to notice that a lot of things you are doing around some fears is almost second nature to you, hang out with the fact that you may be living IN fear where it has control of you and you don't have control of it.

LIVING *IN* FEAR VERSUS LIVING *WITH* FEAR

So how does one deal with Fear? Well, there are actually two ways that you can deal with it. You can either live IN fear or live WITH fear. Let me explain the difference. Living *IN* fear is living a life where everything that you do, whether it is in school, at work or even at home, is going to be informed by your Fear. If you are fearful of speaking in front of people, I can pretty much guarantee that in your life, you are not going to speak up often, or at all because you are living *IN* fear about speaking. If you fear taking risks, chances are you are not going to be one who becomes an Entrepreneur or even invest in high risk stocks. Why? Because you are living IN fear, and this fear guarantees that every move you make is going to be informed by your fear. That DJ on your 24/7 personal radio station will not just have its own show, it will own the entire station, meaning you will hear it all the time. You will call into the show asking fear personally "how do I handle this?" Fear will love you for asking, and then give you an answer which is usually based *IN* fear.

Now living *WITH* fear is another story. As I mentioned earlier, there is no way of getting around it. It will always be there. However, to live WITH fear is living a life knowing that Fear will broadcast on your personal radio station, yet you will not be informed by it. You will say to Fear "I know you have an opinion, and I thank you for sharing it, now I gotta go live my life." Living WITH Fear is just that. It is in your life, but it does not rule your life. Fear will show itself. That's fine especially given you know it will be there, but you choose to go on and do what you need to do anyway. So with all that being said I put it like this:

To Live IN Fear = Allowing Fear to inform your choices and moves in life. To Live WITH Fear = Knowing the Fear is there, but you are unstoppable in your actions and do not allow your fear to inform your choices and moves in life. So choose your life, your possibilities and future. Do you choose to live a life IN fear or live WITH fear? When you live a life IN fear YOU pay, but when you live WITH fear, IT pays. You make the choice.

One of the most misconceived notions about life which I can see comes from a state of fear is what it is going to look like if you screw up! For some odd reason, we have been programmed to be PERFECT!!! All the time, every time. You wake up, you look perfect, you go to school, you be perfect, you play on the team, you are perfect. So with that being the condition, we are indirectly programmed to be scared of making a mistake or not looking good, or missing the mark of being PERFECT. Have you ever met someone who was getting ready to take some major action in their life then all of a sudden they stopped and you hear them say "what if I screw up?" I know when I hear that statement I always comeback and ask "what if you are successful and great?" Of course I get this funny look as if to say "wow, I never thought of it that way."

A few years ago I served as an Emcee for the Illinois Leadership Seminar (HOLLA!!!). This seminar provides the opportunity for High School Sophomores to spend a weekend to participate in activities and discussions that include Entrepreneurship, Leadership Styles and Diversity. This particular year there was a participant who I noticed was painfully shy. She didn't seem like she really wanted to be there or have much to do with the entire weekend. That was day one. By the end of the first day, her shyness broke a little bit, but not much. I would kind of joke around with her every now and then just to keep her spirits up. Well, the following night, the day ended with a Talent Showcase. All of the students were invited to share one of their talents with the entire group. Entries are usually made before the weekend comes. This year we took late entries that night. Right before the show started, she came up to me looking like a nervous wreck. When she came up to me she threw me off a bit because I thought something was really wrong.

"Should I do my poetry?" she blurted out.

"Yeah why wouldn't you!"

Nervously she responded "I don't know, I think ... I just ..."

As she was stammering for words I gazed into her eyes to try to search out what she really wanted to say. It was in that moment I saw fear sitting at home in her mind in the front room with the feet kicked up and the flat screen on, all while waving at me saying "I'm Here! I'm Fear! Get Over It!" What was really showing up was the fear of rejection with a side order of not looking good doing her poetry. She continued "I don't like talking in front of a lot of people." "Oh com'on, just do it. Just go up there and do it." I said firmly. After that interaction, let's just say, she was not convinced. She walked off with a dazed and confused look as if to say "how dare you say that to me." She came around to me another time after that and during that time she could barely enjoy the show because she was debating if she should or should not read her poetry.

About 20 minutes later, the next person who was announced to grace the stage, was her. I perked up immediately when I heard her name. I wanted to stand and offer support because I knew she really fought with doing this. When she took the stage, she said to everyone that she usually doesn't do public speaking or even share her poetry. She then took a deep breath, and began to recite one of the most beautiful poems I had heard. I mean, all I could do was stand there with a big smile on my face and tears in my eyes (okay so I am a cry baby).

I was so moved because she not only faced her fear of public speaking, she spoke from her heart. When she finished the poem, before I could even bat my eye, the audience erupted in the biggest round of cheers, screams, and whistles. She even got a standing ovation. They loved her! I joined in on the rally of applause with a big smile on my face.

A few minutes later, I was greeted with one of the greatest looks I had ever seen. I don't know if I should call it happy, shocked, or stoked. So I'll make up a word here and call her all three. Her look was hapshostoked! That was her look. It appeared as if a whole load had been lifted off of her. She almost didn't look the same. She had this look of amazement and magic in her face. I raised both my arms high in the air to symbolize "victory" and told her "see! You did it. YOU did it!" "I did it. Oh my God that felt so good! I can't believe I did it," she replied. Still with the hapshostoked look, she walked on in her bliss. At the end of the seminar, so many participants thanked her for sharing her poetry.

My observation? What would her life been like if she chose not to share her poetry. What if she chose to live IN fear and not WITH fear. On that stage, don't get me wrong, you could tell that she was nervous and scared, but she felt it and did it anyway. Because she lived with the fear and still took action, she opened up a whole new world in her life. As a matter of fact, I am looking at her being on one of my future projects called "Poetically Motivated." How about that?

What's the moral of that story? The moral is there is tool I am going to give you that can assist in temporarily shutting down fear for those important moments in your life.

THE TOOL FOR LIVING *IN* AND LIVING *WITH* FEAR

Living IN fear or being scared all the time is going to assure you that you will live in fear over and over and over again. And don't get me wrong, there will be times when you get scared, but if you recognize that you are scared and move on right after that, you are well on your way to having a great life period.

So what I would like to offer is this tool. (*Insert Heavenly Music Here*) The Antidote to Fear Is 1—2—3—ACTION!

I know to you it may look kind of funny, and that's great, it means that you are interested in using this antidote. I would say ready, set, action, but that would take too long. Just take action. The best way to get over a fear is to take action. Simple ain't it? Yeah right! It is easier said than done, but if you are sick of the fear whether it stems from fear of rejection or fear of the unknown, just take action. This is where the difference comes in. Those who live IN fear, take no action. They just sit there and complain about why they are afraid of something or someone. When it comes to those who live WITH fear, by taking action, they face their fear and do it any way. They may fail or succeed but they are living knowing that they did something about it. When you look at the story above, the only way she got over her fear for the moment was taking action. She did her 1-2-3 which was the nervousness, and feeling the fear, but then she got up there and did it anyway.

Nike coined it best when they said "Just Do It." You will hear at times "Ready—Set—Action." Nothing is wrong with that, however, people will get stuck in the "Ready" and "Set" stage so much that they never get to "Action." Being in school, you are always going to run across times where Fear will pop up on you. As a matter of fact, when you grow up, get the fabulous job, fabulous home, and fabulous car, fear will still pop up on you. But you have the antidote, *Just take action!*

Now here is a trap I want to uncover for you right away. Does the action always have to be right? NO! If that were the case, you would not be taking action, you'd still be in the "Ready—Set" stage of it all. Now, I just need to let you know this, always trying to get it right is a delayed form of fear. Think about it, while you are trying to figure out if is right or wrong, you are not taking action. So in all fairness, you are not doing it.

Look at Edison. If he based his experiments on getting his actions right all the time, we would probably still be using candles to light a room because he would not have taken action to create what we now call the light bulb. All the actions that you take are not always going to be right. And guess what, that is okay. I guarantee you, in life, it is better to have a life with mistakes to learn from than a life with no mistakes and no learning at all.

As a matter of fact, making mistakes can be a gift. I KNOW THAT SUCKS!!! But it is true. I am a Training & Development Consultant, and though I got a great education, I learned most of my knowledge from making some crazy mistakes. Was it easy, fun, fabulous?? Hecky No! Some of the mistakes that I made cost either myself or even the organization some money. However, these were times were I was taking action. Though it was upsetting for me at times, what I did realize is that I was learning. Almost like Edison, I often found ways to *not* produce a result. Now the greatest thing about that, there were times I was able to train others through my mistakes. It is such the "way of the world" sometimes. If you look at your Mom or Dad or other family members, most times, they will share with you their experience so you won't have to go through what they went through. Do we always want to hear it? No, but here is something to consider. Whenever you learn from the mistakes of others, that will shorten your learning curve tremendously. You walk into something with some knowledge of what should or should not be done.

Earlier when I was talking about putting Mentors on your crew, guess who is going to share their with you? They will. I know one of my Mentors gave me a warning about how not to do something. Did I listen? Of course not. I went ahead and did it my way, and did I make the same mistake, of course. So I had to swallow my pride and share with him how I screwed up. The great thing about it was, he told me what I'm telling you "just learn from it and move on."

So with all of that being said, I encourage you to just take action knowing that at times it will be right, and other times it won't, but because you are taking action, your high school, college, work and family careers will surpass what you could have even imagined.

Okay, we are almost drawing to an end. I think this chapter is one of the most important because you have learned how to recognize fear, you have learned that you can either live IN it or WITH it, and you have learned the antidote for shutting the fear down for some time. Take ACTION Baby!

So Don't be Scurred. You have been well equipped to take on this moment in life when it comes for you. Now, with this tool under your belt you are set and ready to go to the next chapter and....

5

Dream on Dreamer

So we have come this far and we are drawing close to the end. However, I do feel like I have saved the best for last. We get to talk about something that has been known to either make or break a man; to build or destroy a nation; to give or take away life. That something is a Dream.

I am quite sure that at some point or another in your life, you have heard of having a "Dream." Unfortunately, I think so many people have been taught to throw that word around without even realizing what a "Dream" really is. It has become a trendy word. Do *you* know what a dream is? Do think everyone has one? Do you think dreams are possible to achieve? Do these questions have you thinking or looking a little bit deeper? Do these questions even phase you? Understand that there is no right or wrong answer to all of these questions. I am not concerned with what is considered the "right" or "wrong" answer. What is important to me though, is knowing that when you put this book down you will walk away having a firm grip and understanding of what a dream is and giving you the tools to make your dream reality. Are you game for that? If so, keep reading, I got some great stuff for you.

WHAT IS A DREAM?

One thing that I love about what I do when it comes to speaking as well as writing, I get the chance to study many motivational speakers, writers, philosophers, politicians and even poets. I get to study them and their beliefs. However, one of the hardest times in research for me was answering this question. What is a dream? I have yet to find someone who speaks directly to what a dream is. After doing this research, I began to understand and realize why the word "Dream" was tossed around without a lot of meaning. So after reading book after book and article after article, this is what I have come to define as a dream.

A dream is a vision that you have in which it exemplifies a quality of life that excites and inspires you and has no limits or bounds.

It's cool to take a moment to read it again. As a matter of fact, read it several times because throughout this chapter, you will be calling upon this definition.

Have you had moments in your life where you just took off in your imagination and saw yourself attending a certain college, having a certain career, driving a particular car, living in a particular home or even living a certain lifestyle? My friends this is not happenstance at all. This is you experiencing having a dream. All of the instances mentioned meet the definition given above. All of the instances are a vision, meaning you see it but have not lived it yet, exemplify a quality of life, thinking on these things can definitely excite you and there are no limits or boundaries to any of them.

I am thoroughly convinced that all of us have dreams. Some of us may recognize our dreams right away and some of us may not. But what I do know, is that there is something that lies in each and every one of us that is so certain, that we just know that it is meant to be. I have had conversations with some of the greatest people in the world from Motivational Speakers to Filmmakers and I have asked all of them the very same question. "Was this your dream?" The response would be "yes." Then I would follow up by asking "how do you know?" The responses were almost identical for everyone. The response was "I just knew it. I knew in myself that this is what I was supposed to be doing." It seems fairly trivial and may even seem hokey to some of you, but trust me, you are in touch with that same self connection more than you know.

How do I know that? There is something that you do in life or someone that you are in life that allows you to feel a certain amount of freedom. It can be anything. It can be singing, writing, painting, talking to others, dancing, helping, creating, loving, and even supporting. For each and every one of us there is that one thing we love to do. When we look at that, you are pretty close to identifying or knowing what you dream is. Now here's a trick. There are things that you are great at, and in some cases you really like to do. Yet, it does not meet the requirements of the above definition. You may be great as an athlete, however, you don't find yourself visioning being a pro-athlete or even in that field. However, what you do see for yourself in your visions or imagination time is you being a Doctor who specializes in Heart Surgery. You see yourself in your scrubs, performing that surgery, and having a conversation with the patient later down the line saying "you saved my life ... thank you." You may be great at something, yet, that something that you are great at may not be your dream.

I'll give you my example. I grew up in a house full of music. My Great Grandfather was a Pastor and also a song writer. My Mom was one of Chicago's youngest and most dynamic choir directors in her day and the rest of my family just loved to sing. For no reason, we would break out in song. It got so bad in our family, that we became known as the family who loved to Eat and Sing. Well growing up around all of this music, and my Mom being my inspiration, I easily followed her footsteps and became a young choir director myself at the age of 12. As the years progressed, I began enjoying working with choirs and teaching music and I got really good at it. My skills took me several places to teach and direct choirs that often always had members that were older than I. To this day, I serve as co-director for an Award Winning Choir here in Chicago.

Given all of that information, you would think that is my dream right? It's not. I love what I do when it comes to the choir. I love being able to take 40+ voices and creating such a beautiful sound that many take notice of. It's great, yet that is not what you will catch me daydreaming about. However, what I will be caught daydreaming about is how to inspire these singers to deliver music in such away that is touches and inspires others. I love being able to experience my purpose in life when I am teaching music. My purpose is to Teach, Inspire & Encourage. I truly have the privilege to be able to do that through my teaching. Even with all of that said, being a choir director has never been my dream. I know that has been the dream some of my family members saw for me, yet not me.

So if you are asking, "how did I find my dream?" You could not have asked at a better time. Let's take a look at that.

IDENTIFYING YOUR DREAM

I am thoroughly convinced that when it comes to identifying our dreams, we have an "AHA" moment. That moment may not always be huge and big. Sometimes identifying your dream can be in the stillest of moments. The way it usually shows up is in the moment of when you have just done something or have experienced something. The best way I can explain this would be to share with you how I identified my dream.

In June of 2000, I had just gone through a very tough transition in my life. I abruptly ended a relationship of 6 years. I was at a point where I wasn't sure if I wanted to live. But I had people in my life who gave every reason to, including my Best Friend Keith. He knew in times like these I would write poetry. So one day he asked me when was the last time I had written a poem? I told him it had been over a year. When I say the hair on my best friend's head stood up and he started growing pointy ears, and it looked like he began to grow razor sharp nails, he gave me this look with his eyebrows turned down so deep they almost touched his mustache and he said "WHAT!!!! ARE YOU CRAZY!!!! DON'T EVER LET ANYONE OR ANYTHING AFFECT YOUR LIFE SO MUCH THAT YOU STOP DOING WHAT YOU LOVE!!!!" And all the capitalized words above were the words he screamed at me when we were at a train stop ... In public ... with people around ... looking at me as if to say "do you want me to dial 9-1-1?" But he got on my case.

Of course I didn't do anything about it and he knew that I wasn't about to do anything about it. So one day out of the blue he called and said, "come go to this poetry slam with me." I said "Oh, that would be nice." So as we talked and I got more information about the poetry slam and he said "by the way don't forget to bring your poetry." "Man please, I don't have any poetry and why do I need to bring poetry if we are just going to see other poets?" His response? You ready for this? He said "You need to bring your poetry because I entered you into the slam. So, pull out your poetry and call me later" and he hung up on me! Can you believe him? I was so upset, scared, confused all at the same time until I didn't know what to do with myself. When it came to my best friend Keith, I could count on him to give that needed positive peer pressure. Of course, I went through all of my works that I could find and they all didn't seem to have that edge that I would need to even be in a poetry slam. So, I decided to write a poem that would meet the standard of the hour. After just coming out of a relationship that was toxic, there was still some residue left around it. I decided to write on "self." Thinking on this I felt like one of the things we do not do is celebrate who we are. So I decided to write a poem based around celebrating yourself and who you are. It was not a poem that tore people down but definitely built them up. The last line of the poem went:

> *So get your favorite glass, pour your favorite drink*
> *and even if you want a few snacks too,*
> *And take this very moment to celebrate the person in your life who*
> *has made it great ... That person is you!*

I guess the audience was a bit taken by the reading because I didn't get an immediate response. I almost thought, "Wow, did I suck that bad?" Then after a few seconds and some crickets chirping in the background, out of no where came this eruption of applause and a standing ovation. I was so shocked, I almost looked at the people like they were crazy, but I was able to turn that look into a humble smile with silent "Thank You's" crossing my lips. Though the audience loved it, I didn't make the finals. That was cool though, because I felt a part of me that I had not felt in a long time. Something in me was triggered, and I didn't know what it was in that moment. It was almost like running across an old friend. Yet, the next thing that happened, I was so not prepared for.

After reading my poem, during the break, Mother Nature had gotten the best of me and escorted me to the little boy's room. As I was on my way out, this guy purposely blocked my way. I tried to duck and dodge and weave my way around him, but he wouldn't let me pass until I made eye contact with him. When I made eye contact with him, his eyes looked red and puffy like he had been crying. I said my usual "hey how's it going" greeting and still tried to make it around him. Then he suddenly said "Thank you so much. I really needed to hear that." He paused. "I was at a crossroads in my life where I didn't think I was going to live see tomorrow, but after hearing your poem, I decided I wanted to live." WHOAA!!!!! I was thinking to myself. Did my words have that much power? And as he said the final thank you I realized that they did. I stood there stunned with this look on my face as if my purpose walked up to me and slapped me. It was my "AHA" moment, and my dream was triggered, that purpose that I felt deep inside. It was then when I *knew* my purpose. And it was then when my dream began. And today, what you are reading is merely a portion of a dream come true.

I shared this story with you to demonstrate how you can have a moment in your life, where you are so clear about what has happened and what your dream is. Then again, everyone's "AHA" moment is not going to be the same. For some it may take events like mine to trigger what you feel is your dream. For some it may come while sitting and watching a movie or listening to some music or even hearing someone speak that will set the trigger off. When you discover what your dream is, you have such a sense of clarity around what you feel. There is an excitement that you experience. On some level it may be a type of excitement that you have never felt before. That moment is so clear that you instantly know what is happening to you. Have you had a moment like this? If not, don't worry, it will show. Even if you feel you may have missed it, I guarantee you, it will be triggered again. As a matter fact, it will continue to be triggered until you stop and pay attention to what that is.

The great thing about a dream is that you can clearly see yourself doing it. It is second nature to see yourself doing or being your dream. Fair warning though, if you have not come across this moment, I need you to know one thing. This moment will only come when you are in action around something. Action meaning you can be physically doing something related to what your dream or mentally stimulated, i.e. you are watching C.S.I. Miami and you see yourself being one of the Detectives. Like anything else in life, your "AHA" moment will only surface in a state of action. If you are sitting around, playing video games all day or just lying around not doing anything, you are not physically or mentally in action. You are just there. If you don't want to know what dream is, live a life of not being in action. It won't be triggered, trust me.

Let's say you are in action and you think you have discovered what your dream is but you are not sure about moment. I have come up with a set of questions that will help you to identify if this is your dream or purpose.

Can you see yourself doing this everyday without pay?
When you think about doing this, do you get excited?
Do you see yourself making a difference in what you are doing?

You would be amazed at how these questions will assist you in discovering your dream. Earlier I mentioned that one of the traps you have to be cautious about is what you are great at versus what your dream is or maybe. The questions above will usually let you know right away if something is *not* a dream of yours. Usually you will know by the first or second question.

Over the next several weeks, I invite you to really inquire about what your dream is or may be. If you feel you have discovered your dream, congrats, you are on the road to living a life of greatness. If you have not, don't fret, that's a great place to be as well. I say that because there are a number of people who are not even interested in discovering what their dream or purpose is in life. Why? It takes time. It takes work. It takes commitment. Sure, the work may seem heavy duty in the beginning. But look at it this way.

> *If you work hard today, know that tomorrow will be easy.*
> *If you work easy today, know that tomorrow will be hard.*

It's that simple. If you take this into account in your entire life, you will save yourself a great deal of unnecessary madness. I have tested this theory over and over again in life, and guess what, it is so freakin' true!

LIVING A LIFE WITHOUT A DREAM

Have you ever met someone who just seems boring? I mean, you look at their life and your watch them closely. After seeing their life, you almost wonder what else do they do besides, get up in the morning, come to school or work, have lunch, go home eat, watch TV, then go to bed. Better yet, what if your life was like that? What would you feel like if you lived this schedule 365 days year? You become this predictable machine. Beware to the one who throws your off schedule and you miss your lunch! Now you have this boring and dull life and now you are complaining about it all the time. Really, take a moment to look at that. Even if you watched a different TV show every night, your life gets dull. Boring! I know this is a very basic example, but know that there are people out there who are not living their life. **They are letting their life live them.**

Do you have to be jumping off of tall buildings and driving race cars to have an exciting life? No. What will make the difference is knowing that you have a dream to pursue. In some cases ... no. let me say in many cases, the work that is cut out for you to live your dream can seem like it will wear you down. It may even seem that in order to accomplish your dream you have to be overwhelmed with all the details. That is such a myth. You would be amazed at the amount of energy that you come up with while pursuing your dream. It's great! You are excited because you are pursuing what you feel to be a your purpose in life. Yes, it will be challenging at times, but in the same breath, it can be crazy fun! I am not going to harp on a life without a dream, because I really feel if you were not interested in pursuing your dream and having a life of greatness, you would not be reading this book. So I'll leave you with this. Can you imagine your life and how fun and exciting it would be, if you had no reason to be here? Think about it.

THE WORTH OF YOUR DREAM

Ok, so here is where we get personal. Let me ask you something. What are you worth? What is your value? What is your value to your family? If you were not here tomorrow, would you be missed? If you left your school, will it have an impact on some of the students and teachers? Are you worth anything? I am laughing right now because I can only wish that I could here your immediate response to the last question. So if I guessed it right, you are worth something right? Priceless right? Guess what, even if you don't think you are know that **you are the first and the last you that this world will ever see or get to know.** So given that fact, I say you are priceless.

So, if you are priceless, what does your dream become when you take it on? Yes, your dream is you. You have seen yourself doing what you love, you are living your life to be in that space, that moment, that time, in your dream. Ladies and Gents, your dream is like you ... Priceless. Do you get if you lived in a house and one day you came home to find it burned to a crisp and all of your things were gone, you would still have your dream with you. You will have that priceless vision that you carry around with you everyday. If you have that my friends, you are set for life. Material things can be replaced. Think about it, everything is replaceable: House, car, friends, girlfriends/ boyfriends ... You can have that again. But if you lost your dream or did not pursue it ... what affect would that have on your life?

We all have been born with an innate sense of living a dream or fulfilling a purpose. That is your gift from your creator. This is the one thing that no matter what, no one can ever take it away from you. It's yours! No one else's! Only you have this vision for *your* life. Through that vision, that supreme gift, that dream, you have the greatest opportunity to be a gift to this world. To be able to live your vision and your dream and be a gift to this world ... Priceless, just like you. Please don't leave without sharing your dream with us.

FROM DREAM TO REALITY:
THE DREAM TOOLS

"So how do I make my dream come true A'ric?" you ask. It is so *Easy*. Fellas, all you do is climb to the tallest building in your city and find the sleeping beauty ... *and wake her up!* Ladies, go bite an apple and your dream will come true! Funny ain't it? If it were that easy, we'd all be living our dream. But, it's more work to it than that so, I have some tools for you. There are four tools in particular that will send you in the right direction to living your dream.

The Dream Tools

1—Share Your Dream

2—Have Dreamer's Sight

3—Seeing & Being

4—Break the Dream Down

Got it? Ok, this is where the fun begins. These are tools that will send you well on your way to make your dreams *come true*.

1—Share Your Dream

This tool will either excite you or scare you. Either way it goes, you have got to share your dream. When you have discovered what your dream is, start spreading the word about this dream. Why? There are actually several reasons.

Reason # 1: You sharing your dream makes the dream real. We get caught up in our heads often. We think, think, think, and think some more. Yet, it is scientifically proven that when you think and speak something, you are more apt to make it happen. It doubles yours chances making what you say happen. A side effect of doing this … you get more psyched and excited about what you are out to do in this world with your life. Excitement is always a great place to be. The more you share the more excitement you cause for yourself.

Reason # 2: Sharing your dream with others will get them excited about your dream. Now, understand, some are going to get extremely excited about your dream. Some will even let you know how honored and privileged they are that you shared it with them. Then there are some who will just look at you and say "okay." Either way, get out there and tell everyone about your dream. This will also allow others to hold you accountable. Let's say one of your dreams is to be a Fitness Trainer. Well if you have shared this with other people, you will have created allies who are going to hold you to that. So if they see you at the Burger Hut and they see you scarfing down a double cheeseburger with extra onions, mustard and ketchup, with a huge side order of cheese fries, they are going to pull your coat tail in one way or another. They may say something like "so are you going to be telling all of your clients they can have this in their diet too?" It may sting when you hear it, but it will also serve as a needed jolt to keep you on the right path towards fulfilling your dream. That is the joy of sharing it with others. And finally

Reason # 3: You give someone else the permission to search and pursue their own dream. This by far is the coolest reason. I say that because when we are living our lives and we are out there sharing with others what our dreams are, that may be the very moment that we trigger them about their dream. In my book that is cool. See by you not being selfish and sharing "hey this is what my dream is" it is almost like giving them a free pass to their own life. You are so inspiring and excited that they want what you have. Some will even pull you to the side and say "hey, how did you discover your dream?" At that point you can say "I read this book by A'ric Jackson *blah blah blah*" That's not required, but what is required, you tell them your personal journey and the tools you used to get to this point. Doing this can have exponential potential and it all started with you. How awesome is that?

So those are the 3 reasons for sharing your dreams with others. The next tool is …

2—Have Dreamer's Sight

No, you don't have to choose between the red or blue pill like Neo had to do in the Matrix (can't you tell I loved that movie). That is a bit too complicated. When it comes to sight in our own lives, there are three ways we look at it. We view life as the Past, Right Now and in the Future. So looking at life is either having already happened, happening now or going to happen. Let's take a look at each of them separately.

Seeing your life with *Past Sight* means you are always seeing your life as the past. Life has already happened. You don't see any possibility of change or improvement. Why? Because it has already happened. Most of the energy is focused on trying to remember what happened and how it happened and why it happened. That's pretty extreme when you look at it. So if a dream is a future vision, how easy would it be to live your dream if you are always looking at the past? You would be in a constant struggle trying to hold on to what has happened and barely leave any room for what can happen. *Past Sight* is not the sight of someone making their dream a reality.

Seeing your life with *Right Now Sight* is truly a huge step above *Past Sight*. Your life is being seen as happening NOW and no other time. Though this is a step up, it is not always the greatest move to see in your life with Right Now Sight. Why? Let's say you are dealing with some crappy grades? That is what you have right now. If you get caught in only seeing this right now, you can drive yourself to be upset or even depressed in some cases because you do not see what can be in the future. You get stuck in a rut of beating yourself up about what has happened, but you really don't forgive yourself, because you only see right now. In some cases Right Now Sight can be beneficial because you may need to take account for what is happening right now in order to plan for …

Seeing with *Future Sight*. This type of sight I call *Dreamers Sight*. Given that a dream is based in the future, having Dreamers Sight is a great tool. One of the greatest things about Dreamers Sight is it allows you to see your dream, and you can work backwards from that point to right now. That allows you create tangible steps for your life. Whether it is to determine what type of grades you need to get in high school and college in order to go into your field of work, you are seeing with Dreamers Sight. Another great thing about it is you get to mold and shape your dream into what you want it to be. It hasn't happened yet, therefore you have a say so in how it looks when you get there. Seeing with Dreamers Sight is going to be your greatest ally and one of your greatest tools when it comes to turning your dream into reality. The next tool is

3—Seeing & Being

Another way to better your chances of reaching your dream is doing what I call *Seeing & Being*. This is another tool that you will have in your arsenal for blazing your path to living your dream. Seeing & Being is simply taking time to see yourself in your dream as if you have accomplished it already. That means, seeing where you are, what you have on, the people around you, or anything of that that will make it a present moment for you. Then when it comes to being, what does it feel like being in your dream? The being is both physical and emotional. Does being in your dream make you feel nervous, excited, or happy? Does being in your dream allow you to feel the weight of a large trophy or how the handshake from the President of the United States feels?

Let's look at a few examples of using the Seeing & Being tool. If your dream is to become an Academy Award Winner for a dramatic performance, see yourself the night of the Oscars. What are you wearing? How are the people shouting out your name? How do you feel sitting in the seat waiting for them to announce all of the nominees in your category? How do you feel when they say your name which follows the statement "And the Academy Award goes to." Feel it all! Don't short stop on this action of reaching your dream. Hear the thunderous applause of the audience! Feel yourself walking up the stairs. Feel yourself being congratulated and feel good old "Oscar" being put into your hands. Feel your heart thumping as you reach for you acceptance speech.

Pretty exciting isn't it! Now how do you think that would make you feel if you took 5 minutes a day to see this happening everyday! It would put some charge into you wouldn't it? Now some of you may be thinking "well yeah, that's for the Academy Awards, that's pretty big." Okay, let's scale it down a bit. Let's take your Trigonometry or Accounting class for example. You know this is a tough class, but nothing would bring you more satisfaction than to ace the final for this class. Okay so let's see it. See yourself getting up in the morning of your final. Feel your excitement about heading to school to take the test. Feel the confident stride in your walk because you know you are about to ace test. Feel yourself taking the test. See the formulas coming to you easily and the answers even easier. See yourself completing the test and feel the excitement of finishing the test, walking up to your teacher handing her the test, and here your voice inside saying "how ya like me now!"

No matter what your dream is, whether it is to win a Nobel Prize or get that summer job, see yourself being there. And on top of seeing yourself where you want to be, feel yourself there as well. Believe me when I say that It's cool. There are Olympic Medalists who have used this technique of Seeing & Being which they have seen themselves winning a gold medal and felt what it was like to feel the gold medal and flowers in hand while standing on the first place level of the three-tiered podium. What's amazing is this exercise has proven that the athletes who have done this exercise, have literally lived what they saw in Seeing & Being. From Jim Carey to Michael Jordan, they have done this exercise as well.

Seeing & Being is one of those tools that will separate the good and the great. The key to this tool is using both of them at the same time. If you just use Seeing, it will not be as effective as using both. Let's say you are in a competition to win a medal. In seeing it, you see yourself standing there with it around your neck. Great visual! However, it does not compare to seeing yourself wearing it, while feeling the texture of the gold medal in your hand, the tears running down your face, and your heart racing and hearing hundreds of people applauding you. Can you feel the difference? Off the chain isn't it? I think so to. So now we go on to the last tool …

4—Break the Dream Down

When we live up to the true definition of a dream, we see a life without limits. We dream big. That's great. Dreaming big is going to require some action. The action is simple. Break your *Big* dream down into *small* goals. To think that you are going to just have your dream without breaking it down is setting yourself up for failure. Breaking the dream down into smaller goals is not only to take steps to accomplishing and/or living your dream, but it allows you to practice winning the game of accomplishing goals. If you go after your dream without breaking it down, you are depending on a one time victory. Generally what will happen if this approach is taken, you do one of two things: One, you would miss the mark of accomplishing the dream and feel like you have been a failure. Or two, you rely on your *Right Now Sight* to guide your through this time and you say "this dream stuff sucks!" You are basing that off of one attempt.

The difference of breaking your dream down into smaller goals, each goal set can either be a victory or a failure. Guess what it's great if it's a victory. It's great if it is a failure. I say that because if you have failed at a goal, it does not mean you have failed at your dream. Setting these goals are very much like gifts on your birthday. You get a gift, it's wrapped up, yet you don't know what you are going to get. Sometimes you open the gift and you like what you got and sometimes you don't.

Another great thing about setting goals is you are building that "action" muscle. If you set goals towards your dream, you are always going to be in action. When you are in action around your dream, you are constantly creating this level of excitement and suspense. Sometimes it will not always be fun, but the hard time will be bearable because you know this is only a step in your dream's direction. Your life is going to be like a game. You are always showing up ready to play not knowing if you are going to win or lose, but either way, you are building that "action" muscle which will show up in all areas of your life.

With that being said, only you will know what smaller goals you will need to set for your Big Dream. Know if you are unsure, here is where the Mentor in your crew will play a great role in your success. Go for it!

So let's recap the Dream Tools:

#1—Share Your Dream

#2—Have Dreamer's Sight

3—Seeing & Being

#4—Break the Dream Down

If you use some of these tools or all of them, and practice them everyday, you will see amazing movement towards your dream. This is you! The only you this world will ever see, so why not go all out and live the life of your dreams. The way begins with the above tools. All of the tools above I have used and continue to use, and I will say, they have truly propelled me closer to my *Dream*!

Can I pose a question to you? What would this world be like if everyone was living their dream? Really, give it some thought. Just take your family for example. If everyone in your family were living their dream, what type of family do you think you would have? What kind of life would your family live? What would holidays be like? We come up in a society today where we are so pressed to get educated to do what makes the most money, so you can grow up wealthy and have lots and lots and lots of money. Looking at this model, I then question, why is it that only 1% of the world is wealthy? When you look at it, if we are told to do what makes the most money, why aren't a lot more people making a lot more money?

After doing some research, I looked at some of the people who are considered "Superstars" in their own right. It appears that they make a lot of money right? After looking into this I started recognizing a similar pattern. A lot of the stars are doing what they dreamed of doing. I look at some of the singers who are really making it big. They are in it for the love of their dream and not the money. However, because they are doing what they love to do, they tend to make a great deal of money because they are really involved and passionate about it. That is one of the great results of living your dream.

Now what if that was you? What if you lived a life day in and day out doing what you loved to do? My love for speaking in front of audiences started off small. I spoke at smaller functions and events. Can I share something with you? I was really close to giving it up. Why? I wasn't making any money speaking. I got so wrapped into how much money I was suppose to be making that I lost sight of my dream and why I was doing this in the first place.

One day I was speaking to a friend and began to share with him all that I wanted to accomplish with my speaking career and he challenged me with a simple question "so why aren't you doing it?" It was hard to give an answer to that. It scared the crap out of me that I didn't know the answer. Again me being me, I dug deep to find out why. Then I took out the video tape of my very first speech at the Illinois Leadership Seminar and it all came back to me. I discovered that my love for what I did would not do me any good if I were just in it for the money. I had to be in it for the love of helping others. After seeing that, I regrouped and focused on my true reason for speaking.

The year following that, I spoke only 3 times. Was I upset? Yes I was but not because I wasn't making a lot of money. I was upset because I wanted to speak more. I think the group I sing with O4C, knew it because anytime I could speak to them, I would. Once my focus was on my love for what I loved to do, it seemed like the universe opened up all of a sudden. The following year, I went from 3 speeches in a year to 12 in 5 months. The amazing thing about all of these speeches, only two of them I booked. The other 10 came from people who just heard about me and they heard that it seemed that I loved what I did up on that stage.

I share all that to share this … Dream On Dreamer. You are so worth the life you see yourself having. What is it that you want to do?

Really? Just go all out and investigate it. To live the life of a dreamer is not the easiest. You *will* be challenged. And some days you will question if this is what you really want. When you hang in there and stay with it no matter what, the rewards it provides are off the chain crazy!!!

Can you see yourself living your dream? You should. As a matter of fact, be your dream. When you decide you are going to pursue your dream, it is one thing, but it is when you commit to being your dream, that doors will begin to open like you would not believe.

See when I decided wanted to be a speaker, I was super focused on the money, the fame, and the fun. When I did that, I didn't get very far. As a matter of fact, my speaking was just okay. But the day I committed to becoming a speaker that would make a difference in the lives of everyone I talked to, my life immediately changed. I left my high paying job to pursue my love and dream. Hear it is two years later, I can honestly say if I died today, I would be one of the happiest men. Since, I have committed to my dream, my speaking business has tripled! Literally! Not only that, because of my commitment to making a difference I oversee a Training Program for Emerging Professional artists. All of which are pursuing their dream. I love training and training ties into my speaking. Since I have made the commitment, my ventures have taken me across the country and even overseas to London & Paris. My life has changed in such a way that it is beyond what I ever imagined.

I am sharing this with you because it is a part of my dream but moreso, to let you know you can live your dream as well.

Can you imagine a life of getting up every morning to go to a job that is something you love to do? How great is that? There will be challenges, but you would be saying "bring it on" because when you are doing what you dreamed you would and you want to be better at it, you welcome the challenges.

I mean look at some of the people who are living their dream—Oprah Winfrey, Beyonce', Michael Jordan, Emeril, Queen Latifah, Tyra Banks, the list could go on and on and on. I am quite sure I can come up with at least another 300 names. But I will say this. One day I would love to include your name on that list.

My goal currently is to reach 1 Million people and help them realize that they are worthy of their dream; teach them how to recognize their dream; inspire them to be their dream; and encourage them to be their dream.

Every moment in life is new. And every moment past is simply that, the past. For every moment that you live make the best of it. It is your life. So since it is yours choose the best life for you. And no matter what …

Dream on Dreamer—Cheers!

Conclusion

So you have made it to the end? You brave one you. I know this book has probably taken you on a roller coaster ride of emotions of laughter and maybe even tears. Either way, I am grateful to you for reading my book. You are reading a dream realized. Sometime ago, people would say to me "you should write a book." What I never told them, that was one of my dreams.

I have to admit that I am literally completing this book on an airplane on my way back home to Chicago, Illinois. Where am I coming from? London, England. It was a early birthday present to me from my father and his wife. (Thanks if you two are reading this, which I know you are). However, I almost want to say to you, you should be thanking them as well. I know it sounds crazy, but let me explain why.

Prior to taking this vacation, I was wrapped in the everyday life of work. Don't get me wrong, I love what I do and I am excited about being a part of the education of others. The down side of it, I had sat the book down. I would see it everyday saying to myself "I'm gonna finish it, I'm gonna finish it" and needless to say that went over a period of months. While in London (and even Paris) I had the opportunity to visit some of the greatest museums ever! I was blessed to be able to see original works by Monet', Michelangelo, Renoir, Degas, I even saw the original Mona Lisa. I had a chance to visit Castles of former kings and queens, even had the chance to walk the streets where some of the most renowned have walked.

My last night before leaving for home, it hit me like a ton of bricks something that a colleague of mine said to me a few months back.

"A'ric what are you waiting for? The **World** is waiting on you." I heard his voice so clear it was startling. I realized in that moment the way that I could share with the world was by completing this book.

5 Things Your Guidance Counselor Didn't Tell You, started off as an idea that seemed great to everyone. However, the more I got into writing this book and just sharing with you my life, experiences and dreams both accomplished and yet to be accomplished I have realized that my dream would not be fulfilled until it was no longer an idea and an actual work. Could you imagine if the Mona Lisa was just an idea and it never came to be?

This book merely offers you some tools on your road to becoming the best you this world has ever seen. With all the movie stars glitz and glamour and music video blingage, it is so easy to get wrapped into what you are suppose to be like. Well in this conclusion, I want to extend a challenge to you. Don't work hard trying to be that person you see on TV or hear on the radio, or even see in school, I challenge you to be the one person that this world has never seen. That one person is you. Touch others by just being and accepting you. In high school there are students who are waiting for someone to stand up and say "this is who I am!"

All of the chapters were not happenstance. From Who's Got Your Back to Dream on Dreamer, each page was written with you being the best in mind. People are going to have their assumption of who you are and who they think you should be. But if I haven't said it already, I'll say it now *"there is one person you lay down with every night and wake up to every morning, that person is you."* There is no one like that. Sure we can use the superstars as guides, but not as duplication material. They want the real you.

It is my intention that when you finish reading this book you realize that life is all about *possibility*. Possibility is a word not used hardly in today's world, but it is often used by those who to *Dream* and become *Dream Achievers*. Please take some of the tools if not all of them and use them to help transform your life, your family, your community, your country, this world.

What are you waiting for? The World is waiting on *YOU*.

Peace & Love
A'ric
The Speaker & Dream Achiever

About The Author

A'ric Jackson
The Author, The Speaker
The Dream Achiever

For the last eight years, people have allowed themselves to be inspired and motivated by the words of A'ric Jackson. His mission is to "T.I.E."—Teach, Inspire and Encourage all those who hear him, and to take the challenge of helping others pursue their goals and dreams.

What began as passionate poetry designed to uplift the spirit has turned into the pursuit of affecting attitudes and changing conventional thought. A charismatic and genuinely heartfelt facilitator, A'ric knows that his "passion and desire for his audience allow him to connect with them while he is speaking."

After realizing how affected his audiences were by the poetry he would share, A'ric began to feel the tug of moving to the next level with his words. Selected as "Best New Speaker" in 2000 by the Chicago Chapter of the International Speech Organization, Toastmasters, this recognition made him realize how much he wanted to pursue this and how much a void needed to be filled with more strong teens and youth across America.

Watching him speak on stage helps you realize why he is such a unique and gifted orator. For it takes a genuine speaker to present information with shared experience, passion to research a topic much deeper, and to share that information with the audience using skills that will make it a memorable and exciting experience for all.

Currently, A'ric serves as a writer for Krave Magazine based out of Houston and Vassar Magazine out of Chicago.

5 Things Your Guidance Counselor Didn't Tell You is his debut book. He is excited about the people this book will reach and already looking forward to writing the next.

Whether it is through his speaking or writing A'ric is interested in reaching the "NOW" generation and letting them know that there is someone who is willing to take a chance on them, encourage their hopes, and give them the tools needed to making their dreams a reality.

A'ric's motto is "You must first learn to love yourself, then, allow others to follow," and he believes that whenever someone takes time out of their life to hear what he has to say, and acts upon what he says, that makes him eternally grateful.

Visit

www.aricspeaks.com

What People Have To Say About A'ric Jackson

... "Aric Jackson is one of the brightest rising stars in the realm of influencing youth to transcend mediocrity. He brings a unique sense of commitment and passion to the notion that fear need not be an obstacle to self-development and personal achievement."

John Alston Ms, CSP, CPAE
Best Selling Author of Stuff Happens (Then You Fix It)

"Praise for A'ric Jackson as he takes motivational speaking into the new millennium. He addresses issues and concerns regarding the future of America's youth and young adults with the innovative in your face approach to living their dream in a very real way."

Elder Elliott K. Sommerville
Shepherd's Table Covenant Church—Atlanta, GA

"As a second year college student, I can easily say that your message is a great influence for people of all ages ... not just high school students. I was very moved by your speech and will certainly be applying what you said to improve my leadership skills."

Ashley Frazier—Student & Volunteer
Northwest District of Student Councils (Illinois)

"A'ric has an unmatched energy that inspires the very soul"

Adam—Student

"Hearing you speak really made me take a good look at myself and make sure to be myself and not be 'scurred." ... Your words have deeply touched me and have changed my life—thank you!!"

Kelly Patton
High School Leadership Seminar Participant

Want A'ric to come speak at your next event?

Bring It On!

For Booking Information Visit

www.aricspeaks.com

TOPICS INCLUDE

Don't Be Scurred!

A real conversation around fear and how it can have a negative affect on school, family, friends and your dreams.

Leadership–You Gots'ta Bring It ON!

Anyone can say they are a leader. But the real question is "what is a real leader?" This speech focuses on giving our up and coming leaders the tools they need to be an extraordinary leader in their schools, communities, families and ultimately, their life.

Join A'ric in making a difference in the world by having him at your next event.

www.aricspeaks.com

978-0-595-46055-7
0-595-46055-0

CPSIA information can be obtained
at www.ICGtesting.com
Printed in the USA
FSHW010904010919

9 780595 460557